A LITTLE BIT COUNTRY—
AND A WHOLE LOT OF CLASS

The Mandrells. They have a closeness and love that's rare in the world of show business. They have a talent and style that makes them among the most sought after and admired entertainers around. From the Grand Ole Opry to the Las Vegas stage, from Texas to Tennessee, here's a complete picture of the Mandrells on stage and off. It is an intimate glimpse into the lives and loves of an incredibly warm and gifted family.

THE
MANDRELL FAMILY
ALBUM

"A beautiful collection of Mandrell memorabilia."
—*This Week*

"Sincere and straightforward: a sure bet for Barbara's fans as well as Louise's."
—*Kirkus Reviews*

Biography and Autobiography from SIGNET

∽ *The* ∽

MANDRELL FAMILY

Album

BY
Louise Mandrell
&
Ace Collins

A SIGNET BOOK

NEW AMERICAN LIBRARY

This book is written out of love for my family, my friends, and all who read it.

All my life my family has encouraged me and told me that there was nothing I couldn't accomplish if I just would try. I know from experience that the love and faith of one's family is a powerful source of strength.

My sister Barbara has always been there through both the lows and the highs of my life. She has never stopped encouraging me or believing in me, and once she said that she would bet her last penny on me. I know that was not an idle statement. My life has been tremendously influenced by her belief in my ability.

Because this book is so special to me, I must dedicate it to one of the most special people in my life—Barbara, this is for you.

Love,
Louise

Dedicated to both the one I first met, whose honesty and beauty led me to know and love the other, with whom I now share all of life's joys, triumphs, and dreams. If I had not known both, I never would have known love.

Thanks,
Ace

CONTENTS

INTRODUCTION

*O*n March 27, 1980, I sat near an emergency room of the Grant-Buie Hospital in Hillsboro, Texas, a community of 8,500, located an hour's drive south of Dallas. It was county fair time, and on this Friday, Louise Mandrell and her husband, R.C. Bannon, would perform at the high-school auditorium. At one o'clock in the afternoon Louise Mandrell's mind was a long way from her performance, now just six hours away. R.C. had been stricken suddenly with an illness—the severity and nature thereof, still unknown. He was in immense pain and had a temperature of 103-plus degrees. While the attending physician, Dr. David Skelton, examined R.C., we waited in the hallway. Louise's face showed her concern and worry.

I didn't realize it then, but I was about to see a part of a remarkable young lady that I had not seen before. I was about to watch a performer come to grips with a nonperforming, real-life situation. She would face a different kind of pressure, and her reactions would tell me a great deal about Louise Mandrell, human being.

As the minutes slowly passed I noticed that Louise was observing every movement around us. She watched the nurses at the admitting desk and was even more closely sizing up each of the other people waiting in that small hall. Her blue eyes stopped when she spotted two obviously distressed elderly women sitting just a few chairs down from us. I could tell my friend was eavesdropping as a nurse advised the women of what was happening in the emergency room next to R.C.'s. After the nurse left, the two were still obviously in a state of panic and confusion, and, suddenly, Louise left her seat and moved down to talk with them.

I didn't move. I would not have thought of saying anything to those women, and even if I had, I would not have known what to say. Still with a mind full of her own problems, Louise got up to see if she could do anything. I was amazed, though I shouldn't have been.

I found out later that the patient for whom the women were anxious was a husband to one and a brother to the other. He had just had a stroke and was in very poor condition. Those women probably never knew the identity of the dark-haired young lady who offered them words of encouragement and prayed with them, but I am sure they'll never forget the moment—I know I never will.

Before our hour's wait was over and we learned that R.C. had pneumonia, Louise visited almost every patient and visitor on the wing. She didn't introduce herself, and most of these folks will never know who she was, but they all seemed to find something in common with her.

Over the years I have found that all the Mandrells seem to be like that. They can relate to anyone, any time, anywhere. I've seen Louise spend hours with retarded children on what should have been her day off. Those visits never brought her any press clippings, her career was no better for it, and the kids were not impressed by who she was. She just wanted to do it.

I have seen countless examples of this unpublicized service

by the Mandrells over the years. I have had an opportunity to see them at their offstage best, and that best is very good.

I have also had the opportunity to see them at their worst. Honestly, they do get mad, they do make mistakes, and they don't always smile. Still their worst very rarely controls the way they behave or how they view life.

Perhaps they have remained this way because they have never been caught up in the belief they were overly important because of a hit record, a television show, or a newspaper story. They simply believe they're important for the same reason all of us are: We are made in God's image.

This book is not so much a family history, though most of that important information is here. It is not really a how-to-achieve-success-and-be-happy manual, even though I believe there is a lot to be learned on that topic here, too. This book is definitely not a finger-pointing exposé of Music City dirt; I know that the Mandrells must know some of the gossip and nasty secrets, but they don't want to hurt people—even people who have hurt them. They just don't talk about such things.

If this book is anything, it is a book emphasizing and praising God, family, and life. The book reflects the personality of the family it presents.

When you finish reading this book, I think you will feel that the Mandrells have become your friends—someone to root for and believe in. You'll have new proof that the good guys can still win.

One final personal note: Thanks, Louise. You've made me believe in dreams again, and I am a better person for having known you.

Ace Collins

Chapter

∾ 1 ∾

IT WOULDN'T BE
CHRISTMAS
WITHOUT YOU

*A*n unborn child is but a dream. On Christmas Eve, 1948, in Houston, Texas, it looked as if the dream of my parents would become a reality. Yet, as so often happens when a dream is exposed to the light of the real world, an unimagined nightmare suddenly revealed itself.

My dad, Irby, had come to Houston, Texas, for a job as a foreman with an industrial painting company. He thoroughly enjoyed the work, but as in all outdoor jobs, Dad could work only when the weather was good. The last year, particularly during the winter months, had brought little except rain which meant no work and, worse, no pay. Added to that was the routine of finishing a job, packing up, and then moving to another location. Though the job was rarely boring, the travel and grueling pace were taking a toll on both him and my mom, Mary.

Dad probably was more used to this lifestyle, since he had traveled extensively while in the Navy. But Mom was different. Until she married at age sixteen in 1947, Mom had lived her whole life in a small Illinois community, which had a popula- tion of just four thousand. Becoming a housewife and moving

Dad and some of his Navy buddies—jamming

constantly from place to place had been challenge enough, but then Mom had become pregnant. During the early months of her pregnancy, she had been very sick and her body probably never adjusted totally to carrying her first child. Even with the short finances and all the moving, though, my father had made certain my mother saw a doctor regularly. This extra sacrifice had been worth it to him; after all, this was to be his first child!

Now on Christmas Eve, the dream of that child seemed threatened. The pregnancy had been rough, but Mom and Dad had never expected anything other than a normal delivery. As Mom's labor had dragged on and on, it had become evident that there was not just trouble, but serious trouble. Mom had been unconscious now for hours, and the feverish activity of doctors in her room had wound down to a near-halt. My father had to face the facts.

"Mr. Mandrell," a doctor said to Daddy, "you well know the seriousness of the situation. I am afraid we're at a loss as to what to do."

Dad heard the doctor's words, but their meaning must have been almost too great to comprehend. The woman he loved was unconscious and in convulsions. The woman to whom he had promised everything that he could ever give now needed far more than that promise. The situation seemed out of control, and prayer was all he had left. In those brief seconds a hundred prayers and a thousand thoughts must have raced through Dad's mind. He needed a miracle, and he must have wondered if God saved miracles for situations like this.

In those moments of crisis it must have seemed like yesterday, rather than sixteen months ago, when Irby had first seen Mary at that small church in Illinois. Playing and singing in church services had always been special to him—those sorts of things really made him feel good about himself. There was always plenty of good people, good fellowship, and good fun.

*The man my mom fell in love
with—Irby Mandrell*

*The woman my dad fell in love
with—Mary McGill*

Yet, that late summer day in Illinois had offered something even more special—the most beautiful young lady he had ever seen. Meeting Mary had been easy because she was the official church hostess, the one assigned to make sure this visiting musician from Arkansas got to know the folks in the congregation. Being careful to be polite (after all, she was the preacher's sister), Irby had spent the next two weeks getting to know her. In his twenty-three years he had never experienced such feelings, and the day to go back home came far too soon. He had left, but promised to return soon for that sixteen-year-old girl.

Mom may have been only a high-school student, but she was no fool. "I'll come back for you soon" was a great line in the movies, but it just didn't wash in real life. The two weeks with Irby Mandrell had been very special for her also, but when he left, life once again turned to studying, roller-skating, working in a café, and spending time with friends. Her heart may have beat a little faster and a smile may have crossed her face when she got a letter from him, but deep down inside I know she didn't believe he would come back.

Six weeks after the young man from Arkansas left, he made good on his promise. He walked into the café where Mom worked, sat down in a booth, and evidently paid for his order with an engagement ring. I have wondered if he asked for "a cup of coffee and the rest of your life." At any rate, once my mom recovered from the shock, she accepted. To be sure, not everyone was convinced that the little high-school honor student should give up everything to marry this outsider. Still, her folks knew their baby girl was right, and with their blessings, she married Irby Mandrell only three months after they first met.

For the first few months, home for the newlyweds was a small apartment in my mom's hometown. Dad went to work in a local factory, and in the evenings the new couple ran around with the local young people. My folks didn't stop to think about the things they didn't have. After all, they had all that they needed for today and they believed that future needs would be filled. Hard work, faith, and love seemed to be their personal prescriptions for life.

Although Dad was happy in his new locale, he had been born and raised in the South and that's where his heart was. So he said "yes" when offered a job as foreman over a crew of industrial painters. Irby and his bride packed their bags and hit the road. (It seems the Mandrells have been working the road ever since!)

Now on Christmas Eve, those happy times that had seemed so free and unending were all in the past. It hardly seemed fair to Irby that someone who had become such an important part of his life should be cut down before he had a chance to share just a fraction of his dreams with her. In many ways his bride was still a girl just standing on the threshold of womanhood.

Fair or not, the outlook was very dim. But Dad was a fighter and giving up wasn't in his philosophy. A great believer in specifics and not generalities, Dad asked God in prayer to give him something to help save his wife. I am sure there were those that evening who called Dad's manner of thinking blind faith, stubborn will, or plain ignorance, because he refused to toss in the towel and accept the facts. Still Dad has never been one to give up looking for a way to do the impossible, and before long his positive attitude rubbed off on others around him, too! Something good was going to happen.

My father was not (and is not) the most patient waiter. The endless drag of time over the last few days, combined with a certain feeling of personal helplessness, must have been terribly maddening. Yet, he hadn't given up, and down deep inside his rugged heart he knew that his and everyone else's prayers would be answered. The sound of a voice suddenly brought Dad's awareness back to the situation at hand. It was a new voice, yet somehow seemed familiar.

"I've just looked in on your wife, and I'm afraid that I must agree with your own physician," said the man. "Your wife's condition is almost hopeless."

The new doctor had evidently been called in for a second opinion. His words did not raise Irby's spirits, but at least he seemed honest. He continued, "Sir, are you scared . . . is there anything that we can do for you?"

"No, I'm not scared, just worried," Dad answered. "I appreciate all your efforts. Believe me, I fully understand the situation."

There was a pause, and then the new doctor asked, "Don't I know you?"

Dad quickly studied the man's face. "Yeah, sure, we were in the Navy together! You and I were stationed at the U.S. Naval Hospital in San Diego. I was in charge of the dressing room in Building Twenty-one, and you were serving your internship."

The singing Mandrells—Dad, Uncle Ira, Aunt Marjorie

The full recognition now hit the doctor: "We did a lot of spinal punctures together, didn't we?" He reached out and shook Dad's hand.

There was now a fresh bond between them, and an ability to communicate that is built only through working with someone. Dad had well-grounded and complete faith in this man.

"Is there anything that can be done for my wife . . . anything at all?" Dad asked.

After thinking briefly, the doctor replied, "Yes, but it still involves some risks, and it means certain death for the baby. Still, at least your wife would stand a chance. As it is now, no one has a chance."

The doctor's statement hinted at hope, and Dad jumped on it. "Well, let's do it!"

"I'll have to get permission from your regular physician." That permission was quickly obtained, and Mom was rushed into surgery.

Stillness and pain had overwhelmed Irby the last few hours, but now with a fresh face there was at least some hope. The spirits of everyone sharing my father's ordeal lifted, and inside Dad started to feel some confidence. He would keep praying for a miracle and, in the meantime, wait for the doctor.

The hours passed. Christmas Eve became Christmas Day, but Dad remained hopeful. Just being told Mom had a chance to live had given him a tremendous boost. The dream of the child was another matter. For months Dad had imagined holding the child, watching it grow, having it need him, giving it all he had, and, finally, letting it become independent. Now the dream had to be put off for a while, and he could only hope and pray that the person he had already held and loved would make it through this ordeal. If Mom lived there would be other children, and he could fulfill those dreams with them. His wife was not a dream; she was alive. If she lived, he would spend his life finding new ways of proving how much he loved her. Christmas would be a day of life. If she died, Christmas would be a day of sadness and loneliness. He could foresee very little joy or giving if he lost her.

As Christmas morning became afternoon, Dad retraced the steps of his life over and over again in his mind. He also thought of different ways he could tell Mom how the child she had carried and for whom she had suffered for nine months had not lived. Others had faced the same crisis, but what had they said? Dad knew he would be happy, relieved, and joyous if Mom lived, but the loss of the child would hit her deeply. He would have to support her and make her understand that everything was for the best. It would be hard, but together they could handle it. With the weather's keeping him out of work and money so tight, maybe it had to be this way.

Dad attempted to convince himself, too, that all of this was for the best. Still, he didn't understand how any of these events could be in God's plan. He worked hard at accepting the outcome, while still desperately praying for certain things. He emphasized to God how much he needed Mom. If that

Instrumentalist of the Year?

was all he could expect, he would accept it. Dad just wanted God to know that he had to have Mom. As the hours crept by, hope may have lost a little of its glow, but faith remained bright.

No one around the waiting area stopped to notice if the sun broke through the rainy skies when the operating room door flew open, but the faces coming out that door could have lighted the entire hallway. "Mr. Mandrell, you wife is weak, but fine," the doctor said. I doubt that Dad heard the next part—about how it would take a while to get her strength back but eventually she would return to top form. Dad's mind was occupied with *she's fine*. The miracle had happened. God had listened.

Dad probably would have just stayed in a relieved, thankful mood for the next several hours even if the doctor hadn't also said, "You've got a healthy baby girl, too!"

The chances of that happening had not even been considered for hours. Such a wish had seemed so impossible that it would have been too greedy to even imagine, much less plan around, or ask for. Yet now, because of an unexpected gift, a miracle, Dad experienced the full joy of what a new life was supposed to mean. The dream was alive.

When the doctor was able to get Dad's attention again, he added a slight note of warning: "Mr. Mandrell, your daughter had an extremely traumatic birth. Her head is very flat-looking, and the forceps we used left a great many scars. She is not a beautiful baby, but she is healthy."

The Bible says to celebrate life, and I am sure there was much celebration on that December twenty-fifth night. There has been much joy ever since, too! Christmas for the Mandrells is a day that reminds us that God's miracles didn't stop two thousand years ago. It is a day when we remember both the birthday of Jesus and the birthday of Dad's and Mom's first child. Christmas for our family is truly a day to celebrate life and to recall how precious life is.

Someone once said that before the first Christmas, there was music but nothing about which really to sing. Then, in a manger in Bethlehem, God gave the world a song. On Christmas Day, 1948, God gave the world someone who loves to sing songs—my sister, Barbara.

*A duet act was acceptable,
but a trio—
that was stretching the act a bit.*

*Music was as much
a part of our environment
as the air we breathed.*

Chapter

∽ 2 ∽

INSEPARABLE

What are the Mandrells really like, anyway? In attempting to separate our onstage images from our "normal" personalities, I've discovered that there actually is very little difference between the two. A critic once said that our NBC television show "worked" because it represented what we were in real life.

My younger sister, Irlene, really is a clown. She is always setting herself up for a joke, and she treats life more like a game than Barbara or I do. She was like this even as a child.

Of the three sisters, I may be the most different offstage because I'm a little quieter and shyer than most people think. Growing up between Barbara and Irlene may have forced me to be an observer, and I do sometimes treasure calm moments away from people—just doing nothing.

I don't know if Barbara ever just does nothing. She has more energy and life than any person I've ever known. In Nashville, they call her the "Straight Arrow" or "Snow White" because she is almost too good to be true. I think I know her better than anyone else, and I know those nicknames fit. She is literally a superwoman, a very hard act to follow. I ought to know; I've spent my life following her!

Barbara didn't start out selfless and perfect, though. As a matter of fact, from the stories that I have heard from my parents and relatives, she was a great deal like the Barbara portrayed in the growing-up segment of our television show. If anything the show didn't go far enough. She did have a spoiled side, and in the early years (before I came along to straighten her out!), she exhibited that part of her nature from time to time.

Because I took my time in coming along, Barbara was an only child for her first five and a half years. She had been blessed with enough energy for twins and had enough curiosity for triplets. Mom had a full-time job just keeping up with her blonde whirlwind, much less doing the rest of her work. Mom must have lain awake nights searching her mind for ways to keep Barbara occupied and out of trouble during the next day. Unfortunately, she too often failed to accomplish this task.

One of the things that made Mom's policing of Barbara's antics easier was that the Mandrell home was a small, two-bedroom trailer. The mobile home and our frequent moves may have made the later adjustments to life on a touring bus much easier for us. Yet the trailer was handy during Barbara's early years simply because she couldn't roam too far out of sight.

Barbara was only seven months old when she began to walk. By walking I mean that she could actually go anywhere she wanted to go. Now Mom *really* had a hard time keeping up with her! No cabinet was safe, no drawer was secure, and no place was off limits to the newest Mandrell. When Barbara was awake she was always in motion, exploring, seeking a new adventure. She had to know what everything was and how it worked.

With a child in the family, Dad decided the time had come to find a job that would guarantee a more secure and consistent place of residence. He gave up his industrial painting, and the family moved to Corpus Christi, Texas, where Dad became a city policeman. The pay was modest, to say the least, and to supplement the family income, Dad moonlighted extra jobs—including occasional duties as a bouncer at dances. His efforts eventually made the little family enough money to buy a small but comfortable house.

Mom was only eighteen when Barbara celebrated her first birthday. Life with a husband and child, housewifing duties, and a job were great responsibilities for someone who was still growing up herself. Added to all of this, she was fifteen hundred miles from her home and family. This had to be hard, but Mary McGill Mandrell was up to the challenge.

Mom was the baby in the McGill family, and like Barbara, she was not supposed to have survived her birth. Against all odds, though, the too-small McGill baby grew into the beautiful young lady from a rural church-going family with whom my Dad fell in love.

Besides her soft green eyes and delicate features, I'm sure the energy that Mom packed into her five-foot frame must have captured Dad's imagination. Mom was a bit shy, but her deep-seated self-confidence never stayed hidden for long. That self-confidence and a very strong faith in God and people had made her special to her friends and family when she was growing up, and it helped her be mature beyond her years now that she was a wife and mother.

Mom and Dad were perfectly matched. Dad was outwardly enthusiastic, a real joker and cutup—the "life of the party." Mom was quieter and more reserved. Their interests were very much the same, and in the late forties and early fifties, those interests centered on their bouncy blonde Barbara.

Barbara did her best to stay the center of attention, and in the process, she complicated my parents' lives. It was just her nature to be precocious, and in many cases she went too far. Before she reached her second birthday, she had a vocation— furniture restoration. In the five minutes that Mom was out of the living room one day, Barbara discovered a can of lard in the kitchen and smeared a thick coat over the couch. The result was horrible, and it took Mom days to clean up the mess.

Barbara and her favorite cop—Daddy

Barbara jumped next into sports. Throwing things was her specialty, and it looked as though she would one day pitch for a softball team. Around the house her throwing was kind of cute, but when she found a larger field of play, the joke soured. One day in the middle of city traffic, Barbara picked up Dad's billfold, which contained all of the family funds, and tossed it out the window of the moving car. Another party fielded the billfold, and the following week was a lean one for the Mandrells. For a while I'm sure Dad would have welcomed making Barbara one of baseball's first high-priced free agents.

When Barbara stopped throwing items out of the car, she started throwing things in church. During services she often flung her bottle onto the hardwood floor. The glass bottle sometimes broke, creating a nice white puddle that Mom frantically mopped up. After a few services and a few bottles, this became a great embarrassment to my folks. Church had always been one of the few activities that they could go out and enjoy together. Now their daughter was putting a damper on this.

During this time period Mom and Dad first noticed Barbara's interest in music. She hummed along with the hymns before she could even talk, and she stared in wide-eyed amazement at the organ and piano and at the choir when they performed. Music captured and held Barbara's attention like nothing else ever had. She was so enthralled that she didn't throw anything during the musical parts of the service.

Because of Barbara's obvious interest in music, Mom began teaching her daughter to read notes and sang them with her, and by the time Barbara was five, she could actually read music. She still constantly got into things, and Mom and Dad had to move at full speed to keep up with her; but now at least they could hear where she was because her voice rang out with the latest songs she had heard at church or on the radio.

Realizing that their daughter had not only a keen interest in music but genuine talent, my folks bought Barbara a small accordion when she was just five years old. The instrument was a twenty-four bass, which meant it had just two dozen buttons on its left side (a full-sized accordion has 120 buttons). As tiny as she was, Barbara needed the smaller instrument,

Mom and Barbara in Corpus Christi, 1952

and as small as she is now, she probably still should use a twenty-four bass model! Mom showed her how to play it, and within months, Barbara was entertaining visitors at the Mandrell home. The more she learned, the more hooked she became. Music became a way for her to grab attention in a positive way—it certainly beat breaking bottles in church! Much of her energy was now consumed by practice.

With Barbara's lively spirit requiring less attention, Mom and Dad decided it might be nice to have another child. Hopefully, the next one would not have quite as much energy as Barbara. Mom became pregnant in the fall of 1953.

Barbara was not thrilled with the prospects of sharing her life with a little brother or sister. She enjoyed being the only child and saw no reason to change things. Since the latest problem now was how to get Big Sister to accept the expected bundle, Dad began telling Barbara about her new baby and how much fun it would be. But he never fully convinced her that a little baby would be a great addition to the family.

On July 13, 1954, I arrived in Corpus Christi. I suppose Dad may have been disappointed for at least a second or two when he heard the baby was a "she," but when he saw me, I know he was thrilled. Barbara had been through so much trauma during her birth that she was scarred and not too pretty when Daddy first saw her. Mom had an easier time with me, and I was a "beautiful" baby, or so I've been told.

With Mom and me both in good health, the time quickly came for us to leave the hospital. The only problem was introducing Barbara to another girl in the family. Mom and Dad wanted Barbara to accept me on her own. Dad developed a plan. Now many people who deal with Irby Mandrell strictly in a business sense might not realize that he is quite a card. He loves to kid and tease, and he enjoys setting people up for harmless little jokes. What he did on July 16, 1954, was set Barbara up, but not so much for a laugh as for a way to show love. When Mom and Dad brought me home from the hospital Barbara was still unconvinced that I was necessary. Nonetheless, she was a bit curious.

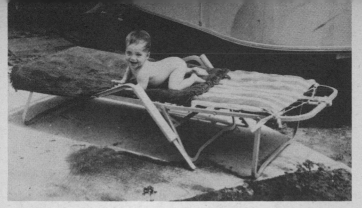
Here I am doing my "bearskin rug routine"

When the car pulled up into the drive, Dad got out, picked me up, and stormed into the house. He marched right past Barbara and didn't stop until he reached the bathroom door. There he turned and said to my big sister, "This can't be our baby; it's a girl! We don't need another woman in this house, so I'm going to get rid of her." With that he closed and locked the door behind him.

At first Barbara was confused, then she panicked. She hadn't even seen the baby yet, and now her father had decided not to keep it. She pounded her small fists on the door and begged Daddy to reconsider, but, through the locked door, she heard the toilet flush. Soon afterward Daddy strolled out empty-handed and said, "That takes care of that."

Barbara rushed past him and looked into the empty commode. Then she heard a sound. Turning around, she saw me resting safely in a bassinet. She stared wide-eyed and breathed a sigh of relief. As Mom and Dad walked back into the bathroom, she reached to pick me up. With their help she did.

More than two decades later Barbara recorded a hit song entitled "Hold Me." That song may have been written about a woman and man in love, but when I first heard it, I thought of that bathroom scene in Corpus Christi. Barbara started holding me there, and she has been ready to hold me whenever I needed it ever since.

An official family portrait before Irlene

Mom and Dad's psychology had worked. Barbara shared some of her spotlight with me and immediately became a caring big sister. Besides helping to change and feed me, she sang to me and played her accordion for me. She also took great pleasure in showing her baby sister off.

I was a more average baby than Barbara had been. I had my looks to get attention, so I walked and talked at a more normal age. I know Mom was relieved. I was a good baby who caused few problems and headaches. I would make up for that as I grew older.

Meanwhile, Dad found that serving on the Corpus Christi Police Department was something he really enjoyed. He was constantly exposed to new and different situations and had many chances to serve people.

Dad's becoming a cop had changed Mom's life. Now she had to deal with his ever-changing shifts and had to wonder if Dad were safe or in some danger. With two young children to love and care for, she really needed his strength and his love and asked God to watch over him.

Barbara loved Dad's occupation. She constantly got her way when playing with the neighborhood kids by using Dad's job to her advantage. Her favorite line was, "If you don't play the games that I want to, my Daddy, the *cop*, will come get you in his patrol car." This worked well for Barbara until one of the kids squealed and word came back to Mom and Dad. This time the *cop* came for Barbara and she gained a full understanding of what the long arm of the law meant!

I, too, was enthralled with Daddy's job. I've been told I loved to play with his handcuffs. Once when Mom was bending over to change me, I swung them very hard and hit her in the head. For days she thought that my blow was the cause of her dizziness, but instead she found out that she was pregnant again. This news really threw Barbara for a loop because for a long time she had been convinced she should be an only child. She had finally decided that a duet act was acceptable, but a trio—that was stretching the act a bit. Mom and Dad questioned the timing too. I had been planned, but this one was a big surprise!

On January 29, 1956, Ellen Irlene Mandrell finished out the additions to our family. Barbara, who was still helping take care of me, now drew double duty. She adapted quickly to the new task, fixing bottles, changing diapers, and rocking babies to sleep. At only eight years of age she was efficient enough to allow Mom more rest than normally would have been expected. She was as much a little mother as she was a big sister.

We might have stayed in South Texas for the rest of our youth had a new police chief not been hired in Corpus Christi. The politics of the force changed, and Daddy didn't feel his new boss would back the men up in tough situations. Daddy resigned.

Within a few months of Irlene's birth we packed our belongings in our old Cadillac and moved to Lancaster, California, where Dad went to work as a security inspector at Edwards Air Force Base, after being informed that at the age of thirty he was too old for the police department in California.

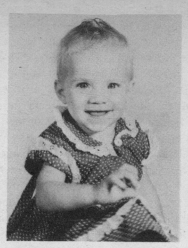

Irlene made us a trio

Financially, things were much rosier for us in California, and before long we bought a new black Volkswagen beetle. It soon became apparent that in order to haul all of us in the VW at the same time, we would need the specially made luggage that fits in the bug's unique trunk. The folks decided to buy these pieces and, after leaving Barbara and me with a neighbor, drove off with Irlene to the car dealer.

Traffic was unusually heavy that day, and the wind whipped the little car all over the road. Suddenly, Daddy swerved to miss a truck, and the VW lurched out of control, slid into a ditch, and started rolling. When it stopped, resting upside down, all of the windows were broken, and Daddy was no longer inside.

Daddy pulled himself to his feet, realizing he had an injured arm or shoulder. Still, his primary concern was Mom and Irlene. He scrambled to the vehicle before the wheels had stopped spinning. Mom was still in the car, motionless. She apparently had been knocked unconscious. She started coming to as Dad pulled her from the vehicle and laid her on the ground. He then reached in to get Irlene—but she wasn't

Daddy the motorcycle cop in Corpus Christi, 1955

there. Frantically, Daddy searched the vicinity. Seconds passed. She wasn't anywhere around the car.

Suddenly, a muffled cry came from under the hood of the VW. Bad arm and all, Daddy lifted the front end and pulled Irlene out from underneath. He was glad the car's engine was in the rear. By this time other motorists had stopped to help. One man offered to drive all of them to the hospital, and Dad quickly loaded the family into his car. This "good Samaritan" happened to be a priest.

As they rode to the hospital, Dad evaluated their injuries . . . Mom had a few cuts and bruises, but apparently nothing too serious. Dad knew his arm was injured, but that seemed to be all. At less than a year of age, Irlene could not tell anyone what was wrong with her, but obviously she had a broken leg and some cuts and bruises. Daddy was most concerned about injuries that might not be visible. With these thoughts spinning through his mind, the ten-minute ride to the hospital must have seemed like an eternity.

The doctors' examination did show that Irlene had a severe concussion. Hopefully, this had caused no brain damage. Her

The Mandrell VW before the wreck

leg was also a major concern to the doctors. At her age the cast and the way the leg healed could affect coordination in her legs. Only time would tell if either injury would have any permanent effects. All of us were very thankful that everyone had survived the wreck. We were even more thankful two days later when a hard rain filled the ditch. If the accident had happened then, Irlene would have surely drowned.

The next few months were traumatic for my folks, and they prayed that their daughter wouldn't be handicapped by the accident. With each passing day it was obvious that Irlene was responding normally. When the doctors cut the cast off and examined her one final time, they assured us that both Irlene's head and leg had healed perfectly. We still tease Irlene by telling her, "In retrospect, your *leg* did heal perfectly!"

The Volkswagen episode was just the beginning of a series of accidents for my little sister—"the perils of Irlene." She always seemed to find new ways to injure herself, and in the process cause us all a lot of concern. In fact before I entered

The Mandrell VW after the wreck

grade school, I already had saved her life. Well, actually, if it hadn't been for me, her life wouldn't have needed saving. The story goes something like this.

When I was five and Irlene four, we were quite resourceful at inventing toys and games to amuse ourselves. One summer day I found a clothes basket and some rope, and, by tying the rope onto the clothesline, made a swing. I thought I had invented the best ride this side of Disneyland.

I enjoyed my new invention. Finally Irlene asked for a turn and I climbed out. As it turned out, I should not have given her a ride. Somehow, the support ropes became tangled around her neck, and when she fell out of the basket, she ended up "hanging" in mid-air with her feet dangling above the ground. Choking and gasping, Irlene couldn't scream—but I made enough noise for both of us. I also grabbed her legs and tried to hold her high enough to ease the tension of the rope. After what seemed a lifetime, Mom heard my screams and came out and untied my little sister. Irlene survived with only some nasty rope burns. My swing quickly became a clothes basket once more.

Another of Irlene's disasters began when she fell while skipping down a grass hill. She broke her arm, and if the break had been a quarter of an inch closer to her elbow, bone growth would have been hampered and her left arm would have been shorter than her right. Fortunately, she once again healed perfectly, and Irlene's drumming career wasn't cut short before it even began.

Later, when Irlene was barely school age, she had another of her accidents. This time she was playing with the little boy across the street and a stray dog roamed into the yard. The boy decided to throw a brick at the dog and scare it off. Irlene came to the dog's defense, dived between it and the flying brick. The dog emerged unharmed, but Irlene was not so fortunate; the brick split her forehead open.

Head wounds usually bleed a great deal, and this one was no exception. By the time Irlene got home, her face was covered with blood. Mom washed her face and was shocked by the sight of the white, exposed bone of Irlene's skull. Mother rushed her to the doctor for stitches. At first Irlene's scars were gruesome, but eventually they were concealed in her hairline. Obviously, they don't show now. I've always believed that Irlene is the truly beautiful Mandrell sister, but during her early years she gave me no competition for the family beauty title. It was hard for Irlene to be beautiful in bandages!

Except for the trauma of Irlene's injuries, our preschool days were very normal, at least until Barbara had put in a few days at school. She came home, got out flash cards, put up a portable chalkboard, and began to teach us things that we would need to know for our first few years of grade school. She took her role as "Little Teacher" almost as seriously as she did those of "Little Mother" and "Big Sister." Irlene picked up on these lessons more quickly than I did and would later prove to be a much sharper student when she started school.

Even though Barbara genuinely enjoyed having her little sisters around most of the time, we did have differences of opinion. Mom and Dad didn't allow us to argue for very long. They would hear out all sides of the dispute, and then they would make what they considered a fair ruling. Once they had been forced to intercede, we didn't question the final judgment. If we couldn't solve our problems on our own, outside authority had to rule. The only thing that further pleading on the issue got us was some punishment.

Mom and Dad were always supportive and very fair parents. They worked long hours and extra jobs to make sure that we girls had the needed material things. We always had food, clothes, and a warm bed. More importantly, though, they were excellent in dealing with our spiritual needs and took the time to teach us how to get along with each other. They would interrupt their own busy lives to read us stories, listen to our stories, play a game, or listen to our good-night prayers. Mom and Dad always seemed to be there, for all the little things, as well as the big ones.

We tended to do more things together than most families did. Sometimes it certainly would have been easier to leave the kids at home while shopping, but we usually all went together. Mom and Dad really tried to find family activities, even though for them it meant giving up going to a show in order to take us to a carnival or a parade. Because of all the time we spent together, I think Barbara, Irlene, and I felt we were important and contributing members of the family.

Music was definitely a key to this family togetherness. With Barbara practicing her music or playing a new song on the record player, we were almost always surrounded by music. Dad would entertain us with his guitar, and his brother, Uncle Al, would fascinate us with his drums. Music was as natural a part of each day as television was for other children.

When we traveled by car we almost always sang together. We probably didn't sing any differently than most families, but I think we did sing more. Maybe it was easier to sing than to listen to three girls argue over who would sit by the window or to hear us ask "How far is it now?" My favorite song during those long rolling performances was "Smokey the Bear."

A stop on the way to California

As a family, we also went out of our way to keep up with relatives on both sides of the family. Many miles were put on our various cars between California and Illinois and Arkansas. We developed a true sense of who we were by meeting and visiting with family members who had come before us. These wonderful relatives would later become our strongest supporters as we struggled to get started in music. They often drove many miles to see us entertain, told hundreds of people about us, and gave us the moral support we needed to continue. They were also supportive when we struggled with problems in life. Many times special relatives helped me through a heartache or enabled me to understand better an illness or a death.

This attentive support, security, and love provided by family members created a sturdy foundation of confidence and assurance, even when we were small children. We knew we were part of a team and understood what that meant.

Barbara, Irlene, and I were raised with the philosophy that God was first; the family, second; and the individual, last. My parents not only taught us this, they lived it. Not surprisingly one normal and important family activity was family prayer. Usually this was done around the table. Church was our main source of friends, fellowship and, most importantly to us, music. Finally, whenever we girls had a need or a problem, Mom and Dad asked us to talk to God. The way that Mom and Dad talked about Him and with Him in prayer, caused us to accept the Lord as a Member of our family.

Dad had put himself last many times by working extra off-duty police work to make our Christmases and birthdays more special. His dedication to us and our needs made finding out that there wasn't a Santa Claus much easier, because I loved Daddy for all the work he had done to give us a Santa all those years.

Another important thing my folks did was always attend school or church programs. Little things like that proved to us that they really cared about things that seemed big to us.

An important feature in growing up in the Mandrell home was that my folks seldom embarrassed us in front of other people. If we were running wild or showing off in front of visitors, Mom or Dad would call us aside and privately warn that our actions would be dealt with in due course if we didn't straighten up. "Due course" meant "after the company leaves," and the family was alone. All of us had some "due course" and were spanked or disciplined in private. But though we may have embarrassed ourselves in front of others, Mom and Dad hadn't added insult by coming down on us then. This policy showed understanding for our feelings, and I will always respect my folks for it.

With the preschool teaching Barbara had already given us, Irlene and I had a head start when we started school. I also had an added advantage that even Irlene couldn't boast of. The year before I entered the first grade, I had introduced myself to the faculty, students, and the entire Lancaster Parent Teachers Association (PTA). I also had made my stage debut that same evening.

The first-grade class was performing a few Christmas numbers for the PTA one December evening, and the entire Mandrell clan was watching the show. (At least most of us were watching the show. *I* couldn't see anything over the heads of all the people in front of me.) A nice man sitting next to us suggested that I go up front where I could see much better. I walked the length of the aisle, climbed the stage steps, and stood beside the last little boy on the stage. When the first-graders concluded their numbers, I followed them off the stage, sharing their pleasure with the loud applause. Mom was embarrassed, Barbara and Dad were amused, and Irlene and I wondered what all the fuss was about. I still think my "performance" should have earned me some credit towards the next year's studies.

A typical first child, I suppose, Barbara was always a good student. For starters she worked very hard. Because of her self-discipline she made excellent grades and had no difficulty in school. I was more of an average student. I didn't have any real problems, but didn't learn some subjects as quickly as Barbara had. Thankfully, Mom and Dad didn't pressure me to be as quick as Barbara. They accepted the fact that we had different strengths and weaknesses and only asked me to do the best I could.

Irlene was a different matter, taking school by storm. She was such a quick learner that she gave reading exhibitions, won school poster contests, and had counselors and teachers wanting her to skip grades. She remained with her age group, though, and because she wasn't forced to excel, she grew bored. Learning was just too easy for her, and she suffered from a lack of challenges.

For all the studying that Irlene didn't have to do, I had to do double. I admit it—I hated homework. I particularly resented staying indoors working on school lessons while "speedy" Irlene went out to play. To encourage me to do my homework and to help me learn, Mom invented games for me. She would plan drills on state capitals, multiplication tables, or spelling similar to television game shows. I was the guest, and she was the host. When I gave the right answer, she rewarded me with praise. When I really knew the material well, I got to show off my knowledge to the entire family. I didn't know it then, but Mom actually was teaching me to compete against myself. I was the one who pushed myself to learn. And, ultimately, the family's attention and praise was the reward that kept me working and learning more.

Mom always was a "pro" at making learning fun. Once, when she became concerned that Irlene and I were drinking too many soft drinks, she set up an experiment for us. She placed a nail in a glass of soft drink, then showed us later how the nail had rusted. The lesson was: What the soft drink did to the nail, the soft drink will do to your insides. The experiment would have accomplished Mom's goal if Irlene hadn't wanted to see the same thing done with a nail in a glass of water.

Undaunted by this one failure, Mom continued to use psychology to help us learn the lessons of life. When we felt we were being treated unfairly or felt sorry for ourselves, she would remind us of the biblical story of Job or find an article in the newspaper about someone who really had it bad. We then accepted our little problem and figured out a solution.

Mom also stressed that each of us would be able to do anything we wanted to if we would dedicate ourselves to doing it. This approach worked in many areas, from learning a Bible verse for Sunday school to making an A on a test in a hard subject. Mom believed we could do it, and often just her belief was enough reason to work to achieve the goal. Many times Mom acted as both our coach and cheerleader. This direction and support probably helped build the confidence we showed later onstage.

When Mom was too busy or Dad was at work, the responsibility for keeping an eye on Irlene and me fell back to Barbara's small, but able shoulders. Barbara was a unique

Trying to convince Santa we had been good girls

combination of lady and tomboy. She took a great deal of care in how she looked, how her hair was fixed, how she walked, and how she talked. But she also was an aggressive member of all the pick-up baseball and football games in the neighborhood. Even at age nine Barbara somehow combined the social graces of a woman (enjoying the attention and favors they provided), with the rough-and-tumble, go-for-the-victory attitude of a boy. She already felt that no task was too big and that she could do anything.

When Barbara did meet someone who could beat her in a race or on a school project, she did what was necessary to improve herself and her abilities so she could win the next time. As competitive as she was, though, she respected her elders, minded her place, and was very polite when the situation so required.

Sometimes Barbara seemed a bit bossy when she dealt with Irlene and me, but we really didn't notice or care. We practically idolized our big sister, and whatever she wanted to do was fine with us. Usually this meant that Barbara planned musical productions so that Irlene and I each had a part. Barbara was an organizer, generally knowing exactly what she wanted for our little home productions. Years later when we had our television show, I remembered the home productions Barbara had directed. She still had the same energetic imagination and the ability to picture how the talent on hand could make something turn out.

Even when we had barely begun to walk, Barbara had Irlene and me performing by clapping our hands. Later, we progressed to beating sticks or toy drums, and holding hands and skipping. Finally, we graduated to singing simple songs and backed Barbara up when she needed added voices for her numbers.

When our home talent shows became more spectacular, Barbara would usually play the accordion or a small organ while she sang. Our top "billing" every year was at Christmas, and Barbara would rehearse with us for weeks. Our Christmas audience was a very special one. Besides our usual crowd, Mom and Dad, we could expect a few relatives and close family friends. This was the *big* time.

Barbara costumed us in our best dresses, and if she could find three that matched, so much the better. She wanted the show to have a uniform look and feel, and she wisely picked out songs with words we could remember and some sort of common theme. Of course, we always prepared an encore number just in case we had an enthusiastic "house."

I doubt that our shows were anything special, but they were original. Our audience always responded with applause, and we began to love the sound of clapping hands. I have a hunch that even then Barbara was already dreaming of becoming an entertainer, but Irlene and I were just enjoying the momentary attention.

Mom and Dad faithfully continued to provide musical instruments and lessons for Barbara—and later for Irlene and me. This was all Barbara really needed, because she had plenty of enthusiasm and the natural talent to play almost any

Even in grade school Barbara had that confident look

I was as shy as I looked in this school picture

instrument she touched. By the time she was ten, she already had guitars and amplifiers, and they received more attention than her dolls. I find it hard to remember a time when Barbara wasn't playing an instrument or singing a song. And when she wasn't doing either of those, she listened to music or watched music shows on TV.

Music was as much a part of our environment as the air we breathed. Dad and Mom had both grown up singing and playing instruments, and when we kids were still small, began inviting friends over to pick tunes in our family room. Most of these friends were just people who loved music, but some were professional musicians, like Uncle Al, who played drums and had a band. Barbara began to play in these sessions too. She was learning music at a rate surpassed only by her interest in it. She was building on the musical foundation Mom and Dad had given her and expanding her musical talents far beyond anyone's dreams.

By this time, Mom and Dad had made music their vocation

Irlene without any bandages or injuries

as well as their recreation. Dad had become a sales manager for the Standel Amplifier Company, and music was putting the bread on the table.

About this time Barbara became consumed with a desire to learn the steel guitar, and Norman Hamlet, who later was internationally known as Merle Haggard's steel player, became her teacher. When Dad had first met him, Norman was playing at a local club on weekends. He was also having to stay in a motel because his job at the club was over a hundred miles from his home. Daddy and Norman soon became close friends, and Dad invited Norman to stay with us when he was in town.

Our home had always been full of friends and music but now, more than before, our home was almost always filled with people, music, and fun. I doubt there could have been a happier or more fascinating home as the 1960s began. Still, none of us could have guessed what the new decade would bring and how music would soon change our lives.

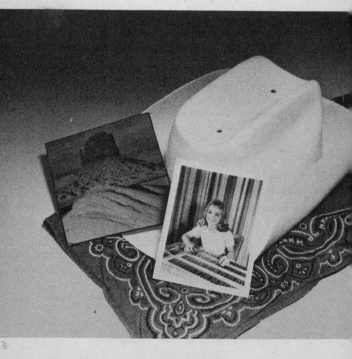

Chapter

∽ 3 ∽

SHE WAS COUNTRY WHEN COUNTRY WASN'T COOL

*W*hen my parents went into the music business, selling amplifiers and instruments on a full-time basis, an entirely new world opened for us girls. Giving three music-loving girls access to music equipment was probably better than giving us free run on the Sears Christmas catalogue. Barbara, then eleven, was old enough to understand the tremendous opportunities. The excellent musicians who bought instruments and equipment from Daddy were, in most cases, very willing to show a new lick on their instruments to anyone who asked. Barbara asked plenty of questions and learned much from the answers.

Norman Hamlet may have started out just showing Barbara a few things about the steel guitar, but by now he was really giving her lessons. As if this challenge were not enough, she signed up for the school band and began practicing on her newest instrument, the alto saxophone. On both the steel and the sax, Barbara learned the fundamentals quickly, and the people who jammed at our house, her band director, and Norman Hamlet were all amazed at her speedy progress on both instruments. It was obvious to everyone that my big sister had some amazing talent.

When Barbara wasn't practicing her music, she devoted her time to excelling in other activities. She was the star sprinter of her junior-high track team and set school track records that stood for years. Had she not become totally involved with her music career, I am sure she would have continued in organized athletics in high school. Twenty years later, on ABC television's "Battle of the Network Stars," she proved that her athletic abilities were still remarkable. Howard Cosell was impressed with both her speed and her competitive spirit.

Even in junior high Barbara would push herself to exhaustion to win a race. She trained harder than anyone else on her team. In practice sessions, she ran extra dashes and distance races to get in better shape, and she ran home, to the store, or anywhere else to supplement her training. I push myself hard, but nobody pushes as hard as Barbara. She stretches herself beyond the limit.

When Barbara worked on her music, she practiced for hours each day. To her this was more important than television or dolls. Many times she played until her fingers were numb. She had such a desire to be good, to be the best, she often refused to quit practicing even when her hands ached or her mouth was sore. She had Daddy's confidence and drive, and Mom's abilities and desire for perfection.

While Daddy guided, provided for, and entertained the family, Mom worked behind the scenes in some very remarkable ways. She was our teacher, our best friend, and our playmate. She could adapt herself to any situation, could seemingly be any age, and could do anything we needed done. One minute she would be a best friend, talking about dolls, school, or boys, and the next minute, the world's greatest mom, motivating us to study, practice, or clean up our room.

In high school Mom had been an honor roll student and a member of almost all the school's organizations. Many of her teachers were just sick when she announced she was leaving school to get married, and the teachers had tried to talk her into waiting until after graduation. Love won that argument, and she left. But just because she left high school didn't mean that she'd ended her education. She continued her studies on her own to improve and expand her skills while working as a secretary. She excelled in shorthand and typing, as well as being a good bookkeeper, budget planner, and office manager. To this day she still keeps the books, answers the mail, and runs the family office. Mom is the one we all turn to when some task needs to be done efficiently and right.

The most remarkable of Mom's abilities is that she can sit down and teach herself how to do almost anything. She first finds the proper information, then trains herself. Most recently she has started on the computer, but back in the late fifties and early sixties, one of the skills she developed was music.

Mom's ear for music had always been good, and she had learned to play piano and read music in church. Still, she wanted to know more. She read and studied music theory, and later she passed some of what she had learned on to us. With her ability to store and use knowledge and her talent at making learning fun, I believe she would have made a great teacher. Mom is just one of those rare people who bring out the best in others.

Mom ran the household much like a business, with organization, fairness, and high productivity. We girls got along very well together because she taught and expected us to do so. The team attitude was strong but our individual personalities were allowed to grow. Still, respect for and consideration of each other's needs were stressed. Mom and Dad didn't let us walk on one another.

Looking back to childhood, Barbara, Irlene, and I cannot remember Mom and Dad arguing. I know they had their problems like all other couples, but they were not discussed in our presence.

I remember when Barbara entered junior high she seemed to think she had graduated from being a child; that she was mature and sophisticated. Irlene and I didn't fully appreciate or recognize this change, and this was a source of great frustration for Barbara. She constantly insisted that we treat her less like a child, and more like an adult. All of this came to a head one evening when my parents were entertaining some company. Barbara wanted to spend some time alone in her room, and Irlene and I wouldn't let her. We kept barging in, begging her to play with us, asking silly questions, bothering her dolls, books, or anything we could find. Try as she would, she couldn't redirect our attention and became totally frustrated. Irlene and I should have seen, from the look on Barbara's face, that she was very put out and left her alone. But we continued to pester her until the visitors left.

Barbara grasped this opportunity to deal with her two little sisters and marched to the local law enforcement authorities, Mom and Dad. She stated her case: "These children are totally out of control. I cannot believe that you allow them to treat me or anyone else the way they do. Believe me, when I get married and have kids, they will never act this way. And if they ever do, I'll spank them."

Barbara was proud of her statesmanship, and she was equally proud of being able to relate the present situation and her own future as a mother. With a slightly smug look on her face, she waited for Dad to take action against the guilty parties. Irlene and I thought that Barbara had made a good case, too, and were preparing to make a quick exit to our room. Maybe if we did an extra good job in cleaning it up, our sentence would be light.

We were all shocked, Barbara even more than Irlene and I, when Daddy suddenly grabbed Barbara, turned her over his knee, and began to spank her. Not since have I seen Barbara's blue eyes as big as they were during those brief moments, and Irlene and I started to really enjoy this punishment. Then I noticed that Dad wasn't really serious. He stood Barbara up, looked her in the eye, and said: "That spanking was for even thinking about whipping my grandchildren." Then he laughed.

When Dad turned to Irlene and me, we knew we should

*Irby and his angels (note Barbara's first
steel guitar to the left)*

have gone to our room when we had the chance. He didn't
spank us, but we got a firm lecture on respecting the privacy
of others. We later discovered that when we did leave Barbara alone for a few minutes, she would wonder why we
weren't bothering her and would come play with us.

At the time Barbara was to begin her first year of junior
high, our parents went to the Palmer House in Chicago to
demonstrate equipment at a music convention. Dad had decided that the best way to display their Standel amplifiers was
to play music and let the public and dealers hear the quality
for themselves. This was not a novel idea, but most groups
weren't made up totally of family members and didn't have a
steel guitar player who was just eleven years old.

Mom, Dad, and Barbara made plans for their trip to the
Windy City. Barbara was very excited. She has always been
a natural ham, and this was an opportunity to perform to a
new audience. Irlene and I were too young to realize the
significance of this business meeting. We were just overjoyed
to have a chance to stay with our grandparents in Illinois who

spoiled us royally. We loved them dearly and felt sorry that Barbara would have to work. We thought she would miss all the fun.

The trade convention always hosted a large number of fine instrumentalists, such as Chet Atkins, Julian Thorpe, Speedy West, and Joe Maphis. Joe was a well-known double-neck guitar player and a legend among country guitarists. He was representing Echo Fonic Equipment. Dad had met him in California and had been impressed by his talent. He always used the best musicians and was a "class act." At the time Joe had his own television show and played the scores for several popular TV shows and movies.

Playing before such well-known and talented musicians would have frightened most amateur musicians, but Barbara seemed unbothered. Maybe he was too young to suffer from stage fright, but I have a hunch the prestigious audience did not faze her.

Indeed, Joe Maphis was very impressed with the Mandrells' little steel guitar player. She was cute in her frilly dress and white flat shoes, but most of all she was an excellent musician. Joe had to know more, so when he asked Daddy who his steel player was, Daddy proudly replied, "That is my oldest daughter."

"Well, Irby, how old is she?" Joe asked, a puzzled look on his face.

"Eleven."

Joe was surprised not only by Barbara's musical competence but also by her stage presence and poise. She was pretty and talented, and when Dad introduced her to Joe, he discovered she was charming and polite.

Joe left but could not get Barbara off his mind. A short while later he found Dad again and asked if he could hire Barbara to be on one of his upcoming shows. The particular date he was thinking about was in July in Las Vegas at the Showboat Hotel and Casino. Joe and his wife, Rose Lee, would be appearing there with a great lineup of country

Mom, Dad, and Barbara with all her instruments, 1960

talent, including Tex Ritter. Dad had surmised that Joe had been impressed with Barbara, but he was still quite surprised.

Dad discussed the idea with Mom, and then Barbara, who was very excited. Mom and Dad wanted, in every way they could, to give her a chance to display her talents, so they knew that they couldn't deny her this opportunity. And the new exposure might bring in some additional business. Dad decided he had to accept Joe Maphis's offer. Barbara squealed with delight.

Only a few days after demonstrating equipment at the Chicago trade convention, Barbara was in Las Vegas at the Showboat ready to display her own talents and personality. She was no longer just Barbara Mandrell, junior-high student; now she was "The Sweetheart of the Steel." Most kids would have been overwhelmed, but not Barbara; she just wanted to be worthy of that title.

"The Sweetheart of Steel" blowing them away with her sax

Mom and Dad had total confidence in her. They had witnessed her dedication firsthand and believed she could handle the pressure of a top show and a paying audience. Barbara had a childlike faith that she could do anything and that all of her dreams would come true. She had worked hard and was looking forward to her debut in the "Entertainment Capital of the World."

Irlene and I were too young to go see Barbara perform that first night, but we were excited simply because she was. She had told us what this big event meant to her, and we were looking forward to having her tell us all about it. With a new dress and some very pretty white shoes, with her hair in long curls, and with a determined look on her face, Barbara met the audience. Her face was serious and studious as she played the first bars on the steel guitar. The notes were perfect, and as her confidence grew, she looked up at the crowd and smiled. She knew she had them and also sensed she had what it takes to be a performer—a feeling that comes from deep in your heart, and as intangible as it is, lets you feel at home onstage. At that point the audience becomes an ally and friend, not the opposition. This audience was rooting for Barbara, and she knew it.

Her performance ended and Barbara left with the lovely sound of a standing ovation ringing in her ears. Her hard work had paid off. A career had been born. The newspaper reviews were great, and so was the pay—three hundred dollars a week. She made sure she was paid in real silver dollars placed in a money bag. She then took them to the hotel room, where she was staying with Mom and Dad, and counted them over and over again. Those silver dollars made quite a heavy load, but they stacked higher than bills did and were a tangible sign of her earnings. Barbara's attraction to the silver dollars soon diminished, but her affection for the audience and their applause grew with each performance. The money was nice, but having people cheer for you was better. When the Showboat Hotel asked Barbara to come back and perform for five hundred dollars a week in December, it was the thought of hearing the applause again—not the money—that made waiting for the next show so hard for my big sister.

When Barbara came back from Vegas she was still the same sister we had known before she left. She did tell us what it was like to play before big crowds and showed us some silver dollars. Eventually, she had some publicity pictures made, but she acted just as normal as ever and didn't seem like a star to us.

Barbara's practicing had become such a normal thing that we didn't consider it unusual for her to be in her room for hours playing the steel, sax, or banjo. It was also common to have weekend jam sessions with ten or twelve different local musicians at our house. To us this was how the typical American family lived. Our family wasn't "Father Knows Best," but it did resemble "Ozzie and Harriet." Of course our father went to work; I don't think that Ozzie ever did!

When Christmastime came and Barbara and the folks returned to Vegas, Irlene and I went to our Aunt Wanda's in Phoenix. We couldn't think of a better time than Christmas to be spoiled at her house. Our own family was to celebrate Christmas after the other three came back from Vegas, but Irlene and I knew we would be able to con Aunt Wanda into an early one just for us. So we weren't too overly concerned when Mom, Dad, and Barbara left for Vegas.

The stars on the bill at the Showboat now included Red Foley and Gordon Terry. Red was famous for the songs "Peace in the Valley" and "Old Shep." He was Pat Boone's father-in-law and was one of the most popular members of the Grand Ole Opry.

Gordon Terry was one of country music's greatest and best-known fiddle players. Later he would influence my fiddle-playing style, as well as the way hundreds of other fiddlers "saw" their instruments.

This time in Vegas Barbara not only impressed Red and Gordon, but with her talents and energy she caught the eye of a new host of fans and critics.

Back home again Barbara continued to perform on a Los Angeles-based TV show, "Town Hall Party," a program on which she had first appeared earlier in the year. That TV show became *the big break*, as now millions of people had an opportunity to see and hear her. Irlene and I were impressed, too. Being on TV made Barbara a "star of sorts" in our minds.

Barbara enjoyed doing the weekly live TV shows. But at home and school she was just another twelve-year-old kid. Except for her hours of practice, she was like any girl on the verge of becoming a teen-ager: She camped on the telephone, went to slumber parties, and beat up any boy who challenged her. She really had the best of both worlds.

Although Barbara wasn't overly concerned about such matters, "Town Hall Party" was having an effect on her future. Through television Barbara was being exposed to not

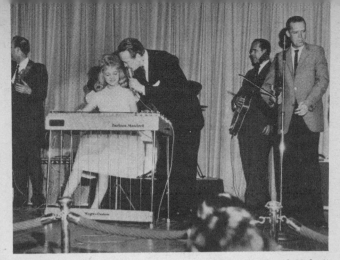

Barbara with Red Foley in Las Vegas (Photo by Frank Valeri)

only the general public, but to promoters, musicians, and big name show business acts. Many of these people contacted the television production company and the local station to find out how to employ this talented blonde "sweetheart." The phone at our house began to ring more, too, and soon my big sister was working during her school vacations and on a few weekends.

At this point Barbara could have halted the whole thing by simply telling Mom and Dad she wanted to be a normal, unemployed twelve-year-old again, but she didn't. Mom's and Dad's lives probably would have been easier if she'd done so. Suddenly they had to be booking agents, managers, musicians, itinerary coordinators and, of course, parents. Still, if Barbara wanted to give music a stab, they wanted to give her every opportunity to succeed.

While Mom and Dad pledged themselves to helping their oldest daughter succeed, they also made every effort not to let guiding a budding star's career complicate our home life. One way they kept Barbara's feet on the ground and her mind in touch with reality was by leaving her enrolled in a public

The music store in Oceanside—Daddy with business partner Bill Hendrick

school and expecting her to do well. Barbara knew that if a choice ever came between her grades and her career, the stage would take the back seat. So she had to keep studying. The folks also encouraged her to participate in many activities. This way she expanded her mind, met new people, and was exposed to a variety of things. Barbara sang in the glee club, was first-chair saxophone in the school band, and joined various clubs and organizations. She still found some time, too, for Irlene and me. Looking back on those days, I wonder when she found the time to sleep.

At this time my parents bought a music store in Oceanside, California. The music store was to us kids what a candy store would have been to most other children. Every imaginable "toy" could be found there. What more could any child desire? Everything there made noise! Oh, yes, 1962 and 1963 were beautiful years—from my point of view, anyway.

For Christmas 1963 my parents gave me a beautiful new accordion. With its ivory-and-black keys, its black-and-silver body and red trim, I thought it was the most beautiful thing I had ever seen. It was a 120 bass model, and I was as totally consumed by it as Barbara had been by hers before me. I now felt like a real part of this musical family, and I may have envisioned myself becoming the "Sweetheart of the Accordion." Lawrence Welk had better watch out, because I was on my way! I made Mom sit down and give me my first lesson that night, and by the time the evening was over, I was picking out simple tunes. With Mom's instructions, whole new horizons opened to me—all through this one small accordion.

Irlene didn't show much interest in music, and it appeared at the time the second family musician to follow in Barbara's footsteps would be the last. Mom and Dad certainly didn't put any pressure on Irlene; if she weren't really interested in playing the accordion or anything else, that was fine.

The next musical instrument challenge Mom and Dad gave me was a drum set. I learned fairly well, and I was the only drummer in my third- and fourth-grade classes. Still, I was better on the accordion; I wanted something that played tunes.

Irlene, though, was fascinated by the drum's rhythmic beat. She played on the set from the time that they came home, and soon she was showing not only interest but real talent so Dad and Mom arranged some lessons for her.

Irlene was not quite as quick on drums as she had been on school work, and I must have been a bit pleased with that. After all I wanted occasionally to be better with at least one or two things than one of my sisters. Still, Irlene did learn fast. One day she came home from a drum lesson and seemed very discouraged. Mom went over to her and asked, "What's wrong, honey?"

The little green-eyed charmer looked back and said, "I just can't learn this new stuff."

"Now, Irlene, remember what your father and I have told you about looking at things in a positive manner. Think positively!"

Without hesitation, my little sister replied, "I have been. I am positive that I can't learn it." As usual, Irlene was just kidding us, and she went back to her room and worked on her drums until she had learned her lesson.

Irlene and I also became involved in extracurricular activities besides music. Irlene's centered around art and reading, but mine was gymnastics. Gymnastics offered me a chance to excel in something in which no one else in the family was involved. While I could perform only at school or PTA programs, I still felt very talented and important. I received great encouragement from home, and had we not moved away from the program or had not music become such an important part of my life, too, I think I would have continued to compete in this sport. Like Barbara, I loved the challenge of any kind of competition. Plus, gymnastics was an area where I could compete against myself.

While Irlene and I were going about becoming more artistic or graceful, Barbara was spending more and more time playing the steel guitar. Her school vacations were now totally devoted to touring with different road shows as a special guest star.

One of the first major stars she worked with was Johnny Cash. He seemed quite taken by her, and through his shows, she had a chance to perform before thousands of true country music fans. Johnny and Barbara remain close friends today.

Another star who became not only an inspiration to Barbara, but a friend, too, was Patsy Cline. The friendship with Patsy had been almost instantaneous, their personalities seeming to mesh perfectly. Patsy loved to have Barbara on the road with her, because at the time in country music there were very few female performers. Barbara's company may have been a nice change from all the men Patsy normally traveled with. Finally, there was someone to share "girl talk."

Barbara must have thought of Patsy as the kind lady she wanted to be. Patsy could sing any song well, and she was very much her own person. I also think Barbara enjoyed doing things for someone who was older. After all, Barbara had always been blessed with only younger sisters. Many times when they traveled together in early 1963, Barbara fixed Patsy's hair and helped with her makeup. After shows

"The Man in Black"
(Photo courtesy of Johnny Cash)

she got to stay up late and hear stories all about the business.

Barbara's last two-week tour with Patsy was a gold mine of exposure, education, and thrills. Their friendship grew in spite of the differences in background and age. Patsy seemed to believe that this little blonde would be going somewhere in the business and wanted to help her. Barbara became closer to Patsy than to any other entertainer she knew at that time, and when the time came for my sister to return home, neither she nor Patsy wanted to part. Barbara called Daddy and asked if she could stay and work with Patsy just one more week. If she stayed, she might be able to play the Grand Ole Opry with Patsy. No one wanted to have a daughter work the Opry as much as Daddy did, but he had already allowed Barbara to miss several days of school, and education had to come first. The answer was no. Patsy could introduce his daughter to the

Opry on another occasion. So, on an early March day, Barbara packed her bags and returned home.

As disappointed as she was about not getting to tour another week, Barbara was filled with excitement about the two weeks she'd had. She told us about the crowds, her numbers, but mostly about Patsy. We could tell that she was looking forward to working with her again.

On Wednesday, March 7, 1963, we learned over the morning radio news that Cowboy Copas, Hawkshaw Hawkins, and Patsy Cline had died in a plane crash near Camden, Tennessee. They were returning home from a benefit concert that they had performed in Kansas City. Ironically, the benefit was for a family whose musician husband and father had been killed in a car wreck. If Barbara had stayed and worked the Opry that weekend, she probably would have gone to the benefit, too. She might have died in the plane crash, or maybe Patsy would have taken a different way home. None of us will ever know.

On Saturday, March 10, the Grand Ole Opry stage was silent for one minute as each member of that organization, the audience, and those listening on radio remembered their friends. That silent sixty seconds has been called the saddest moment in the history of country music. At our house, it was one of the saddest, too.

At the time, Irlene and I were too young to fully understand death. We saw and felt the reactions of Mom, Dad, and Barbara, but we didn't understand death's permanence or question why it had to happen. But Barbara must have asked why. Still, she had been blessed to share some moments with a legend, and more importantly, to share some dreams with a friend. God may have taken Patsy Cline, but not until Barbara had been blessed just by knowing her.

Looking back, we learned at least two lessons from that plane crash—time is a blessing, and people can have a great effect on others in even a short amount of time. Barbara was now determined to make her time count.

She was no longer
just Barbara Mandrell, junior-high student;
now she was
"The Sweetheart of Steel."

Suddenly they had to be
booking agents, managers, musicians,
itinerary coordinators and, of course,
parents.

Chapter

∽ 4 ∽

ROMANCE

Mom and Dad now knew for certain how much Barbara wanted a career in music. Performing with entertainers such as Joe Maphis, Tex Ritter, Merle Travis, Gordon Terry, Patsy Cline, Red Foley, and Johnny Cash had given her an even deeper devotion to music, and as her keen interest had increased, so had her personal drive. Capturing that drive and channeling it into the most productive areas of achievement became a goal for Daddy. He knew Mom and he had to be careful not to neglect their parental duties while Barbara went on lengthy tours.

Daddy concluded that Barbara still needed her parents nearby—to help guide her, to help her grow up in the music business with as little pain as possible. She was just too young to be expected to be an adult. So, Daddy formed the Mandrell Family Band and got back into performing music in a big way.

In the new band Mom played bass guitar, Daddy was the front man, singer, and rhythm guitarist, and Barbara played steel, bass, banjo, and saxophone. To fill out the group they added a young man named Brian Longbeck on lead guitar,

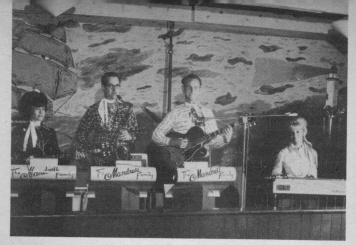

The Mandrell Family Band—Mom, Bill Hendrick, Daddy, and Barbara

and a good-looking twenty-two-year-old named Ken Dudney on drums. Ken was quite a cutup and clown. Irlene and I loved him.

The Mandrell Family Band played mainly on weekends, in a radius of about 150 miles from home, at armed forces bases, or at clubs that catered to men in uniform. In California, there were large numbers of both. A typical concert consisted of popular country songs, instrumental numbers, a few jokes, and several old standards. It was the same basic show routine bands had used for years and still use today. The big difference in our band was that women did more than just sing. The rarity of having females play instruments, and play them well, made the Mandrells unique.

The servicemen who came to hear the band were a very important audience. Not only were they polite and enthusiastic, but when they went back to their homes throughout the U.S. or were transferred to other bases, they took the story of the band and its little blonde musician with them. While the band thought it was just playing a few dances at a few clubs, its reputation was spreading and a foundation for the future was being built.

The band's weekend schedule did cause a shift in our normal activities, and Irlene and I spent many Friday and Saturday nights with babysitters. A lot of our friends did the same thing, but their parents didn't go to work, but rather went to see people like my parents work. Staying with babysitters wasn't all that bad. Many of our sitters had brothers and sisters our age to play with, and one of them even had horses for us to ride. Irlene and I looked forward to these weekend experiences.

Our family finally moved to Oceanside to be nearer the music store. Our house was painted in natural shades, mostly grays, and to me it was unusual and beautiful because of its many glass windows and doors. The sun always lit up the rooms. We had a glassed-in porch, and Irlene and I loved the small lemon tree that grew in that porch. We could hardly wait to pick the lemons every year.

With the music store, the family band, and three girls in school at the same time, our home was a constant whirl of activity. Irlene and I always had friends over to play, Barbara and her girl friends talked about boys in her room, and musicians would occasionally come by for a jam session. We were never bored, but the place was noisy! If you were in need of some peace and quiet, you would not have wanted to come to our home. But even with the running in and out and all the people—and maybe because of both—we all got along pretty well.

As ideal as I've made our lives sound, things were not always perfect. Our cars didn't always start, our television tubes burned out, and we did get tired of all the music and noise. We were not as perfect, nor did we have quite as "neat" a life as that portrayed on "My Three Sons."

One night when we had company, Barbara gave up her room and moved in with me, and Irlene moved to the living room couch. I normally slept on the bottom bunk, but Barbara wanted it, and after some questioning, slight bickering, and convincing, I gave up and moved to the top bunk.

For some reason we had not turned the light off before climbing into bed, and we began a little struggle of wills to see who would be the one to turn it off. I stubbornly pretended it wasn't on, closed my eyes, and almost fell asleep. Barbara didn't "buy my act." She said something like, "It's your room, Louise; you turn the light off."

By now I was tired of both the arguing and the light. I also was half-asleep and not thinking too clearly. I got up, but forgot I was on the top bunk. I remembered this minor point after I rolled off the mattress and found that the floor was a bit further away. I landed chin first with a loud crash on our drum set, and if I hadn't already been convinced that Irlene was the family drummer, I was at that moment. Dad hauled my bleeding body to a hospital emergency room for stitches. As I recall, when I got back home, Barbara graciously gave me back my lower bunk.

Another incident that insured our membership in the "Imperfect Little Children's Club" happened one evening when Mom, Dad, and Barbara were playing a military base and Irlene and I were home with a babysitter. We thought that this sitter was really cool, and we wanted to be as cool as she was. She smoked, and even knowing we would get killed if Mom and Dad ever found out, we decided to try smoking, too. Being the good, "cool" sitter she was, she gave us two of her cigarettes.

No matter how hard I tried, I couldn't be cool. I hated smoking. Irlene, though, took to smoking like a duck to water. She didn't even cough. We did decide that one cigarette apiece was enough and gave up smoking, or so we thought. To this day I'm not sure how they found out, but Mom and Dad somehow got wind of the smoking episode. Mom asked me first, "Honey, have you ever smoked a cigarette?" Being an honest, fearful, and maybe-a-little-stupid fifth-grader, I answered truthfully, "Yes."

Then Mom asked Irlene. My little sister figured a total denial would most likely keep her out of trouble. Here I was, having taken only a few puffs, and I was to face justice alone. Fortunately, Mom didn't believe Irlene, and she soon reported for sentencing, too.

The punishment was designed to fit the crime, and at the same time supposed to teach us a lesson. The band's drummer, Ken, worked at a drugstore part-time, and he filled a very special order for my Daddy—some of the strongest cigars the store had. With Mom and Dad sitting in the room, Irlene and I were given one each and forced to light up.

Soon smoke was everywhere, and I was coughing, gagging, and crying. I had hated my few puffs on my only cigarette, but the cigar was murder. Irlene was not coughing at all. Her eyes were not watering, and she even blew smoke rings. She, needless to say, gave herself away. When Mom and Dad finished lecturing us and were sure that we had learned our lesson, they excused themselves to the kitchen and had a belly-splitting laugh over Irlene's performance.

Irlene was the family clown. Her first words had been "Goochie-goo," or, in grown-up language, "Tickle me." Her personality is probably closer to my Dad's than either Barbara's or mine. Irlene just loves to laugh. She was probably the biggest challenge for my folks because they never knew if she was serious or not.

Once, when I was five, I had packed a bag and tried to run away from home. Knowing I would soon realize the error of my ways, my folks had even helped me pack the bag. I had walked about two blocks before Barbara came and forced me to go home. I had been mad about something and had just left without thinking. Irlene would have realized that a comfortable bed, food, and the TV were at home; she would have never considered running away from such luxury. Irlene was independent but not stupid. Irlene was just Irlene, and she was an original—then and now. She is definitely a breath of fresh air.

Mom and Dad attempted to recognize our individual traits and treated us accordingly. We were not forced to dress the same way, eat the same way, do the same things, play the same instruments, or excel at the same rates. We were all allowed to develop our strengths and challenged to improve our weaknesses.

Still, there were times when the same treatment was used to motivate all of us. One of my favorite lines, which obviously has served us all well, was this one from Mom: "If you're through practicing your instrument, you can help me clean up the kitchen." Barbara, Irlene, and I almost always decided we weren't finished practicing.

My parents' philosophy on the quality of musical instruments was a great bonus to us too. They always bought us the best instruments on which to learn. Their reasoning was that if we were playing on good instruments, the learning would be easier; the progress, quicker; and our motivation, higher. We never had to overcome the handicap of playing an instrument that wouldn't have sounded good even if played by an expert. Besides, Mom and Dad didn't have to listen to bad instruments during all those hours of practicing!

Music did occasionally complicate school life. Barbara sometimes had to miss a day or two to play a date. This happened rarely, though, and it had to be a special date for Daddy to let her skip class.

Once a math teacher thought that Barbara should be making an *A* rather than a *B* in algebra. She sent a note home and explained how Barbara could do better if she devoted more time to math than to music. This initial note was followed by another and another until finally a request came for a parent-teacher conference.

Daddy had already talked to Barbara, and she had explained that she knew the basics of algebra, that she was learning what she would later be able to use, and if she had to make a choice between school band or math, she would rather be a top student in band. "Daddy, I want to play music for a living, not teach math," she had said.

On the day of the conference, Irby Mandrell represented the defense, and he wasted no time in asking his first and last

72

The man who discovered Barbara—Uncle Joe Maphis, with his wife, Rose Lee

question: "Is my daughter able to count and figure percentage?"

"Yes," the math teacher replied. "She is very good at that."

Daddy closed the discussion with this summation: "If she can play music, count money, and figure percentages, that's all I expect her to do."

Barbara's *B*s in math were never a problem again, and the notes from the teacher ceased.

A majority of the teachers, school board members, and administrators viewed Barbara's music and her notoriety as something special, so she rarely had a problem with missing school for a tour or making up a test. She was one of the stars of the school band, and the band director on occasion moved a concert date just so she could play. Education can include a great many things that take place outside the classroom, and, if anything, the traveling and stage shows were enhancing what Barbara was learning at school. Most of her teachers recognized this.

With her music career being the one big exception, Barbara was a typical teenager of the 1960s. She loved dating, fast cars, and getting together with girl friends to talk about boy-

A typical teenager of the 1960s

friends. She listened to Beach Boys records, watched "Man From Uncle," and read fashion magazines. Yet with every year the performing she did on weekends and holidays made her a little more mature and a little more aware of the real world than were her peers.

One example of these unique and maturing events began at nearby Camp Pendleton. The Mandrell Family Band had played many dates at or near this large marine camp, and the men in uniform had become some of the band's biggest fans. Seeing all of their familiar faces made the whole group feel very much at ease. A date for them was almost like a visit with old friends.

After one of the Saturday night shows, some drill sergeants asked Dad if the band ever played for private parties. The band occasionally did, and Dad gave them the details. The men then told Dad about their friend whose son was dying of cancer. The boy had heard about the Mandrells and had asked if he could hear them in person.

Dad was deeply moved and suggested that the band could take off an afternoon on the next weekend and play a show for the boy. The marines said it would have to be sooner because the boy wasn't supposed to live more than just a few days.

The next afternoon, the band unloaded its instruments and set up in the living room of a home not much different from ours. The young boy on the couch was obviously tired. His body and face were gaunt, but his stomach was swollen. In many ways he looked more dead than alive. Yet, there was still a sparkle in his eyes, and when the music started, a smile lit his face.

The show was limited to only thirty minutes, and when the band members, the marines, and Mom and Dad left that house they tried hard not to look at each other since they were all crying. I'm sure they thought their gift had been inadequate.

The boy died before the next weekend.

Of all the early dates the Mandrell Family Band played, one of the most prestigious was the Marine Ball in Honolulu in 1964. Mom, Dad, Barbara, Brian, and Ken were thrilled to be asked to perform with Joe Maphis as his backup group. Irlene and I couldn't see what all the fuss was about, but then we hadn't been invited! We would just have to wait at Uncle Al and Aunt Linda's and hear about it secondhand. We honestly figured that Hawaii wouldn't be much fun without us, and Mom, Dad, and Barbara assured us that we were right. They told us that it would be a real "drag" because all they would have time for was work. When they returned Irlene and I were suspicious; all three had beautiful suntans.

Christmas is probably the most magically special time in almost every American family's life. Our house was no exception; yet when we were grade-school age, Christmas Eve was special in a different way. The band would always play for servicemen on that evening, which meant Irlene and I were apart from Mom, Dad, and Barbara on the night before Christmas. We knew that they weren't neglecting us but were giving someone else a taste of family on that night.

Christmas Eve may have been quiet, but Christmas Day made up for it. It was Barbara's birthday, of course, and she didn't let us forget it. She always emphasized that she wanted a gift for both her birthday *and* Christmas, not a combination gift.

With all of those gifts to buy for Barbara, Irlene and I needed to work to earn money. The folks taught us that a gift was something you made with your time or bought with your own money. It was supposed to be something that required some sacrifice. We couldn't earn money by doing chores around the house (those were part of our family obligations), so we had to find outside jobs. Usually, we could rake leaves or clean out flower beds. We found that most of our neighbors were suckers for a cute smile and pigtails.

When we received our "paychecks," it was tempting to find cheap gifts so we would have some money left over for ourselves. But we never could forget Mom and Dad's lessons about Christmas. They taught us that when God gave His Son, He had sacrificed a valuable, precious life for each of us. Therefore, if we didn't give all that we could at Christmas, we knew we wouldn't be very happy or proud because we had not given our best. So, we always figured out a way to spend every penny on someone.

The Christmas gifts we received were always a bit unusual. While other girls were getting play kitchenettes and dolls, we were getting jukeboxes, drumsticks, and musical instruments. We did have Barbie and Ken dolls, too, but they didn't hold quite the significance for us that they did for other girls our age.

I guess that if Christmas meant one special thing it was that all the family sat down at the table and ate at the same time. Because of our varied schedules, we rarely were able to do this simple thing.

Church was the one central scheduled event that held us together as a family. As a small child, I had started out a little leery of church. Every time I received a dime on Sunday morning, Mom and Dad would have me drop it into this plate that was passed around the room. I wanted to keep my dime and being forced to give it up did not seem like freedom of worship to me. After a while I began to enjoy the music part of the service, so I didn't mind losing a dime now and then. Later, when I learned where the money was going, I actually enjoyed giving up my dimes.

All of us girls loved church, and I think that was so because my folks enjoyed it so much. They had met in church, and for generations the McGills and Mandrells had sung, preached, and learned to know God in church. It was a natural part of all of us. We were also fortunate to attend churches filled with people who knew that being a Christian didn't mean you couldn't laugh, smile, and have a good time in life. I think a lot of people and churches have lost sight of the simple fact that God saved us to make a joyful noise and to be happy because we have Jesus in our hearts. I wonder how many souls have been lost because their Christian friends lost real happiness and joy in life? When we go to a church, we have fun! People who can't imagine having fun in church probably have not been to churches filled with genuine joy. By joy I mean the ability to love someone just for what he is that day, not for what he may have been before that day. Joy also means a style of worship in which you get to communicate with God in your own way without being forced to do it just like everyone else does. God made each of us unique, but too often we are expected to be the same and act the same. When that happens, religion becomes a tool of the mind and not an extension of the heart.

Being reared in church and moving from town to town as we did, it's not surprising that Barbara, Irlene, and I became aware of different worship practices. And because we had been raised to be ourselves and think on our own, we weren't too old when we developed different interests in regard to church services. We each wanted a church that fit our beliefs

77

and personality, and we wanted to go to church and worship with our friends. These unique ideas led to unique Sunday mornings at the Mandrell house.

Each Sunday morning, after eating breakfast together, we loaded into the family sedan and drove to the church of our choice. Barbara was dropped off at a church her friends attended. Irlene and I went to our friend Connie Johnson's church. Finally, Mom and Dad arrived at their own church. After the services the pickups were reversed, and over lunch we discussed what had happened at each of our churches that morning.

My folks never seemed unhappy about this arrangement. They were quite happy that we were eager to go and did not have to be forced. Besides, they wanted us to spend time with our own Christian friends—and what better way to do this than by attending church with them.

*Daddy was first in line to congratulate the new
Miss Oceanside*

As each of us grew older, church and the friends and experiences that went with it served us very well. It was easier to know how to behave when you were surrounded by good friends. But equally important was the knowledge we gained that there was such a thing as good, clean fun. Christianity gave us the strength and perception we needed. My faith ebbed and flowed as I grew older, but the basic foundation remained solid. Without parents who had made sure we attended strong churches, none of us girls would have had that.

Barbara remained very much the stereotype of what a good teenager of the era was supposed to be. She read *Glamour*, she enjoyed driving cars, she listened to the radio, she loved to buy clothes, and, like a great number of teen-age girls, she also entered a beauty contest.

Barbara waited until the last day before the deadline to enter the Miss Oceanside contest, and even though she was a very pretty girl, she hardly fit the normal description of a beauty queen. For starters she was short. Also most of the young women who had entered that year, and almost all of the past winners, were at least college age. Barbara was just a sophomore in high school. She downplayed the contest at home and tried to convince everyone that she really didn't have a chance at winning. Yet, I think deep down inside she really thought she was going to win, and onstage the night of the contest, she looked and acted like a winner. Her confidence and poise were obvious.

The night of the pageant, with a crowd of 350 people looking on at the El Camino Playhouse in Oceanside, the mistress of ceremonies, Doris Boyer, announced that two five-foot, seven-inch college freshmen had been chosen first and second runners-up. Then the winner was announced. She lived on Tropicana Drive, she wore a blue pastel formal, and she was my sister. Local critics had already hailed her as the most talented young lady in town, and now the former tomboy accepted the title as the most beautiful.

A later family band shot—Brian, Ken, Daddy, Mom, and Barbara

As Miss Oceanside, Barbara's year of activity included parades, ribbon-cuttings, boat and air shows, and fairs. She managed to attend them all, kept up with school, performed more shows and concerts than ever, and even did quite a bit of dating. Her new title placed her more in the public eye than ever before and her picture seemed to get in the newspaper at least once a week. Her activities enabled her to meet a number of influential people in the area and the publicity aided her musical career.

About this time we noticed that a young musician, who spent a great deal of time around the house, seemed interested in more than just his drums. Irlene and I had loved Ken Dudney since Daddy had hired him as the Mandrell Family Band's drummer. To us he was tall, almost six feet anyway, an older man, and strikingly good-looking—or at the least very cute. And he obviously had good taste, because he spent hours with Irlene and me. He frequently took us out for movies, milkshakes, or ball-playing in the park. He told us jokes, teased us about boys, and bought us gifts for Christmas and birthdays. The only problem with having Ken take us places was that Barbara always tagged along. Try as we might, we could not seem to make her understand that Kenny was all ours.

Then, to make matters worse, Barbara and Ken began to spend more time with each other and less time with us. Irlene and I assumed they were working on music for their act, but in actuality they were starting to make some music of their own.

Mom and Dad had always liked Ken, even though they were a bit concerned initially when their fourteen-year-old daughter had taken a liking to the twenty-two-year-old drummer. Those first months and years they probably viewed it as a teen-age crush that would go away. The main problem with that theory was that the crush seemed to be two-sided.

With the band performing several times a week, Barbara and Ken had to be together a great deal. Mom and Dad became more accustomed to this situation, but I don't think they thought the relationship would be for the long term.

Ken was as imaginative and zany as Daddy, and he took great delight in embarrassing Barbara with practical jokes. During her sophomore year, he always picked her up and brought her home from school. One day he dressed like a chauffeur and borrowed a limousine. As Barbara walked out of school calmly chatting with her friends, a long black vehicle pulled up to the school door and a dapper young man, complete with cap and jacket, jumped out, opened the back door, and said, "Your car, Miss Mandrell."

Barbara wanted to disappear, her friends were quite impressed, and Ken continued to play it straight without even a smile. As Barbara got in, she gave Ken her "drop dead" look. Ken, still standing at attention, just returned her look with a proper smile. Then he closed the door, whirled around the car, hopped into the driver's seat, turned to his passenger, and asked: "Home, Mum?"

For almost two years my older sister suffered through many of these great moments with Ken. She had to look behind every door to see if someone was there ready to jump out and shout boo. Invariably, if she didn't look, Ken was there.

During her junior year, Barbara and Ken decided it would be a good idea for each of them to date others. Ken had enlisted in the navy, and since he would soon be leaving for pilot training, it seemed wise for both to play the field.

I think Barbara enjoyed the phone calls, the flowers, and all the new interest in what she was doing the next weekend. Many of the young men who called were turned down because she was just too busy to date. Irlene and I had a great time flirting with the young men who did come to visit or take her out, but none of them had Ken's special way with us. Barbara must have felt the same way, too, because she seldom saw any of them more than just a time or two. Barbara did have two dates with others that were unforgettable. The first was with the captain of the golf team at high school. His name was Woody, and he was tall, blond, and very good-looking. He also had a new car equipped with everything, including power windows. With his qualifications, Irlene and I had approved wholeheartedly of Woody, but Daddy was suspicious. But, like most dads, he didn't approve of anyone for his daughters.

Woody asked Barbara to go to a movie at the local drive-in—a romantic idea Irlene and I thought, but Daddy didn't feel quite the same way.

At the drive-in Woody wanted to impress Barbara, so he bought her a pizza and a huge Coke. Barb promptly dropped the pizza upside-down on the new car's fabric seats, but Woody still thought his date was so cute that he didn't seem to mind. After finishing the pizza, Barbara began to play with all the fancy knobs on the car. She made the windows go up and down, she pushed in the cigarette lighter, and she adjusted the radio to her favorite station. When she heard the lighter pop out, she decided to pull it completely out. Now

Barbara always completes everything that she starts, but she grabbed the wrong knob and pulled the volume control off the radio.

I can just imagine her saying, "I'm really sorry, Woody. I thought that . . . well."

Woody probably replied: "That's all right, it was loose anyway."

Soon the car became very quiet, and both of them were absorbed in the movie. Barbara had been nursing her large Coke for over an hour, and she still had half a cup left. Not wanting any more to drink, she casually reached across Woody and tossed the cup out his window. Unfortunately she had failed to notice that Woody had already rolled his window up. The half-filled cup bounced off the glass and landed upside-down in Woody's lap. Barbara came home early that night.

The other well-remembered date concerned a curfew. That night Barbara was supposed to be in by midnight. When at one o'clock Daddy woke up and realized he had not heard her come in, he got up to wait. He became very nervous. He would wait for five minutes, then shuffle in to wake up Mom and tell her what time it was. Finally, he just had to *do* something.

"Mary, it is 1:30; I am going to call the police."

"Irby, why don't you give her just a few more minutes? I am sure that she will be home any second."

At two, Dad had had enough. "She is going to catch it for this, Mary. I can't believe that our daughter would do this!" The door slammed as he went out.

Only moments later another person joined him in the living room. "Would y'all please hold it down; I can't sleep with all this racket!" With that Barbara turned and went back to bed. She had gotten home at eleven.

By her senior year, many things were crowding Barbara's mind, like graduation and whether or not she should continue her musical career after high school. She did a lot of thinking and growing up.

Ken and Barbara had stayed in touch, and I knew she

Barbara, Brian, and Dad playing double-neck guitar

missed him. She became very excited when the day of his first extended leave came closer. When Ken finally arrived she seemed like a new person. I guess Ken had become her sounding board, or maybe even her mirror. She could see herself more clearly when he was with her.

The entire family enjoyed having Kenny back; it made us feel like we were whole again. He had spent so much time at our house that when he was gone something was missing. I was not surprised when Barbara and Ken announced that they wanted to get married. Ken asked Daddy for Barbara's hand (Daddy probably wished that was all he would have to give up!) in a very unique way.

"Mr. Mandrell . . . Irby. I really love your daughter, and I promise that I will do everything in my power to make her happy. I am also aware that you and she have planned a career in the music business. I promise that I not only will never stand in the way of that, but I will fully support it."

Grudgingly, Daddy consented. But I know, deep down inside, he really didn't want to give Barbara up.

Barbara was just seventeen, but her experiences had made her more mature than her age indicated. She had worked, traveled, and experienced situations that had forced her to grow up. She knew her mind and her heart, and my parents knew her. They never questioned if she was ready for marriage.

I was thrilled beyond words. I had always figured on taking Ken if Barbara didn't. He was everything I had always wanted in the brother that I had never had. To compound my excitement, Barbara asked me to be a bridesmaid. At the time, this was the biggest and brightest moment of my life.

Barbara believed, despite Ken's promise in his proposal, that her music career was a part of the past. She wanted to be a housewife, although a Vietnam tour was scheduled for just two weeks after the wedding. After that trip Barbara thought she would only play music for her own amusement.

She and Ken decided to get married two weeks before her high-school graduation. Ken could arrange for a short leave, so Barbara found an apartment for them across town and started to prepare it for a few weeks of marital bliss. After those two weeks, she would be off to the Far East, and Ken would be flying navy planes somewhere. She knew that when she got back she could join him.

As it turned out, Ken was stationed in Washington that summer, and the topic of his bride's whereabouts often came up. He got a laugh when he would say, "Oh, while I'm here in Washington, she's in Vietnam."

On May 28, 1966, Barbara became the first of Mary and Irby's daughters to walk down the aisle into the arms of someone waiting to take her to a new and perfect life, as marriage is usually described in Victorian novels. It was a beautiful day to get married, since the weatherman had fully cooperated with the wedding plans. Daddy, who always enjoyed getting dressed up, looked absolutely smashing in his tuxedo. At most weddings there are almost as many tuxedos as guests, but Daddy was unique at Barbara's; Ken and his groomsmen were all attired in naval dress uniforms. It was my first and last military wedding, and even if it hadn't been my sister's, I would have been impressed with the uniforms, swords, and handsome young men.

The wedding colors were green and yellow. Irlene and I were two of the five bridesmaids and wore dresses of light green and carried yellow floral arrangements. Barbara was beautiful with a full white dress and a simple veil. The church was decorated with just a few long candles and tasteful floral arrangements. The simplicity of everything about the wedding ceremony placed the love between the bride and groom as the focal point for the guests. Barbara wanted a beautiful wedding where the commitment of the couple was the thing most remembered, and she succeeded.

Daddy was very proud when the time came to walk his oldest down the aisle. Barbara chose this precise moment to break one of her heels, and with the ceremony about to begin, the procession retreated. The organist began to "stretch," a show business term that means "stall as long as you can, we are having technical difficulties." Five or six men pulled out pocket knives and almost anything else that they could find and tried to fix Barbara's broken shoe. It took all of their combined engineering efforts to accomplish the task in five minutes. The organist continued to play faithfully, and then, at last, it was time to try it again. This time everything was perfect.

I don't remember much about the ceremony, except that all the Mandrell women cried. We were flooded with emotions, all of them happy. The wedding was over too soon and Barbara and Ken were gone, but I knew this marriage was the perfect way for Barbara to leave us. In many ways my oldest sister had been blessed with a storybook life, and this was another perfect chapter in it.

With the wedding behind us, and school out, Irlene and I could now enjoy the long, beautiful days of summer. We

Barbara and Ken's military wedding

looked forward to sliding on cardboard pieces down Oceanside's long, grassy hills, playing softball, and remarrying Barbara and Ken with our own Barbie and Ken dolls. For a while it looked like the closeness we three sisters had shared was now behind us. Barbara's room was empty, and when we saw her, it was in a different light. She was a grown-up woman now and out on her own. We missed her, but came to accept it as just a natural part of life.

At this time Irlene and I didn't know how soon we would all be together again—closer than ever before. It wasn't something we planned for or dreamed about, but just when we were about to finally give up our hold on our big sister, music would come along and tie us all back together again.

But for now, it was just long summer days and cool summer nights.

Chapter

∞ 5 ∞

OVER THERE

*P*robably at no time in this century has our country been more completely divided than during the Vietnam conflict. We were a nation striving to come to grips with a war half a world away; yet through the immediate and graphic reports of the media we had to deal with the war on a daily basis. Actually it was a war that came to visit us every night on the television news.

As a family we were all very aware of the Vietnam War. We lived very close to a marine base, Camp Pendleton, and many of our classmates' fathers and brothers were serving in Southeast Asia. Some of those men did not come home, and others who did were never the same.

Barbara and the band had visited military hospitals, and I had overheard bits and pieces of stories they'd heard there. I also knew kids my age who had lost fathers. Playing soldier was too real for most of us to even consider doing.

In 1966 the Mandrell Family Band first toured the Far East including Vietnam. Irlene and I had stayed behind with Uncle Al and Aunt Linda. For two girls, ages ten and eleven, it had been a great summer filled with swimming, visiting, traveling, and fun. We certainly had missed Mom, Dad, and Barbara for those three months, yet when the hot days of summer had passed we had been back together again and the memories of being lonesome had faded. At that time I hadn't asked them much about their trip because I never expected them to go again. I had been glad just to have them safe at home.

Now, just a school term later, the Mandrell Family Band was to go back on another tour of Southeast Asia. A year older and slightly more aware of the fact that something could happen to Mom, Dad, or Barbara, this time I was a great deal more worried. Irlene and I didn't want to lose them for even three months, but now we were really aware that if something went wrong, we might lose them forever. I had a strong faith that God would care for them, but I also had occasional touches of fear. When that fear crept into my mind, I would attempt to force it out—the old "close your eyes and the bogyman will go away" technique.

With Barbara married to a serviceman, this trip held new importance for her. She hated to be away from Ken, but she could share her feelings for him and her pride in what he was doing with all the servicemen that she would be entertaining. As much as that first trip to Vietnam had meant to her, this one definitely would mean more.

This tour was also significant because it was to be the Mandrell Family Band's last series of dates. Since Barbara had decided to give up her music career to become a full-time housewife, the Asian tour would be her finale.

Daddy had felt certain misgivings about the first Vietnam tour. The responsibility of taking his family and friends into a dangerous situation had weighed heavily on his mind. Still, because he had been stationed overseas while in the navy, and because of his great pride in our young men, he had booked that tour. Now this second one was even tougher to OK. Yet he felt that the soldiers needed contact with folks from back home who cared about them.

No one in the family questioned the right or wrong of the Vietnam conflict. Our main concern was that our boys were there, and because they were our boys, doing what their country had asked, we wanted them to know that we were proud of them. We appreciated their sacrifices and felt this was a way we could thank them.

As proud as I am that the family band made this trip, I am not trying to paint them just as patriotic heroes. An additional reason for their going was that they were paid very well for their time. Still, money really was a minor consideration. The music store, the band, and a vending machine business that Daddy had developed all were doing very well. The family didn't need the money badly enough to justify the risks for that alone. There was a lot of "red, white, and blue" blood pumping through their veins.

The last weeks of school, Barbara's graduation and wedding, and fabulous spring weather had made the time fly by. Before I had a chance to stop and think, Mom, Dad, and Barbara were preparing to leave. My prayers the night before their departure were longer and more personal than ever before.

At 11:00 on a beautiful June morning, the Mandrell Family Band boarded a jet bound for Japan. Even as they were still airborne, Irlene and I were settling into another fun summer with Uncle Al and Aunt Linda. They had planned some very special activities for us, including swimming in their pool,

Irlene and I catch the fish,
Barbara cleans them!

fishing trips, visits to the library, and a special vacation trip. They knew Irlene and I needed to keep our minds on activities and off the band's tour. They had planned very well.

Vacations were something that Irlene and I had missed while growing up. If we traveled anywhere it was normally to see relatives or watch the band work. With Uncle Al and Aunt Linda we took these excursions strictly for fun.

I wouldn't trade those trips with my uncle and aunt, but I also don't think Irlene and I missed anything by not taking vacation trips with Mom and Dad. A vacation is usually a time when families spend more time together—quality time. We always had quality time at home and didn't need a trip to relax or get to know each other better.

Our trips the summer of 1966 sure helped us to know Uncle Al and Aunt Linda better, though!

We went east to Boise, Idaho, where Irlene and I fished for trout. There were so many fish in the pond we couldn't possibly miss catching some. It wasn't a real sporting challenge, but we surely enjoyed ourselves anyway.

We also visited Yellowstone National Park, where we saw beautiful scenery, grizzly bears, and Old Faithful. While Barbara and our folks were showing our boys in Southeast Asia that America appreciated them, Irlene and I were gaining a true appreciation for America.

Even though my aunt and uncle attempted to fill all of our hours, with every summer day we missed and worried about our family a little more. Irlene started to question me about what we would do if they didn't come back, and we both occasionally had scary dreams. Still, we believed God would keep them from harm.

The separation gave me a chance to think seriously. I began to realize that I wanted to be involved in every facet of my family. Music became more than something just to play and enjoy; a drive to achieve new musical goals stirred in my heart. Irlene must have felt the same stirring. We had decided that if our family ever played overseas again, we were going to be so musically sound on our instruments that they would have to take us along. Even before the others left, Irlene and I had begun to feel left out when everyone else was performing. I know I never said aloud, "Music is what is missing in my life," but I knew if I could play well, chances were less that I would have to be apart from my family.

Thanks to my aunt and uncle, Irlene and I were able to capitalize on our decision to become competent musicians. On a weekly basis, Aunt Linda drove me as much as forty miles for piano and other music lessons. Uncle Al spent hours teaching Irlene more about drumming. Barbara might have said her performing was about done, but we didn't believe that our family could stay out of music forever. When the others got back into music, we would be ready to join them.

During that summer our music became very important in our lives. We were almost always practicing and dreaming of what we could do musically, and our tans suffered because of all the time we spent indoors working. Mom and Dad wouldn't have believed our self-discipline.

Still, music was second with us—the most important thing being the letters Barbara, Mom, and Dad sent from overseas. Seeing one of those letters in the mailbox meant that, for one more day, they were all fine. After that relief had sunk in, we relaxed and enjoyed what the letters said. We read them over and over again, and felt as though we were almost there.

In the first letter from Japan, we learned of the long eighteen-hour flight and that, because they had been following the sun, it was still daylight when they arrived. They had seen the emperor's palace and had eaten an Oriental supper.

We could tell that Mom was fascinated by Japan, which was probably her favorite country on the tour. Each evening the hotel maids turned down the beds, and each lady guest was given a freshly pressed kimono. I could tell that this treatment made Mom feel special.

We received several letters from Japan. The band worked two weeks there, and it must have been an enjoyable stay.

They went on tours of the downtown shopping areas, which were called the Ginza, and they were taken out to sample the Tokyo night life. The only calamities were minor ones. Barbara decided that the drummer's (Mark Peppard) blond hair could use a red tint. Barbara, the hairdresser, struck out. Mark ended up with a head full of bright, orange hair for the entire trip. To say that Daddy was steamed is an understatement.

Barbara, the all-American blonde, also accidentally found herself in the middle of a group of Japanese college students involved in an antiwar demonstration. She somehow charmed her way out of that one. We never found out exactly how.

Most of the two weeks in Japan was spent playing two military clubs a day. The band, which included Brian Longbeck in addition to Mom, Dad, Barbara, and Mark, would play shows for the troops. Usually a Japanese house band warmed up the crowd before the family band went on. The house bands were something else. They sounded just like the famous American country stars. Many of them could sing perfectly in English, but couldn't speak the language. Most of them had memorized songs by listening to records. Needless to say, our band heard and answered many requests for specific songs. Hearing a favorite song could almost take a homesick soldier back to the States for a few minutes.

Japan was a great experience for the band, and since we knew it was a safe place for them to be, Irlene and I relaxed during that time, too.

The next stop was Okinawa. The highlights of this stop, besides the fantastic response of the servicemen, were Daddy's being offered a snake soup dinner and Barbara's getting a tropical sunburn. Daddy decided he would pass on the soup, and Barbara passed out from the sunburn. She recovered quickly and did a show the same evening. Knowing Barbara, I bet she picked out a costume that was color-coordinated with her blazing red skin. She always tried to look her best.

After Okinawa came two weeks in the Philippines. The local agent in charge of the tour assigned each band member

Barbara returned from the Far East a "decorated veteran"

a huge bodyguard. These men shadowed the band wherever they went, and eventually the bodyguards became such good friends that they seemed more like tour guides.

Irlene and I were receiving a letter three or four times a week, and the ones from the Philippines were especially exciting. Barbara had visited a live volcano, seen the president of the country, eaten great new foods like fresh coconut with ice cream, and, most exciting, had ridden a water buffalo. The buffalo was working in a field, and Barbara had actually paid a farmer to let her ride it. I'm sure he thought he'd found the craziest Yank. The buffalo was covered with mud, and Barbara was wearing a white jump suit.

Everywhere the band went in the Philippines locals ran up and shook Barbara's hand. The entire population seemed friendly, and the bodyguards were needed just to keep Barbara's new friends from injuring her with their enthusiasm. The funny thing was that most of these people had no idea who she was or what she did. They just knew she was American and cute.

The band performed mainly at Clark Air Force Base and Stangly Point. Before their nightly shows, they also visited hospitals filled with servicemen injured in Vietnam. The war became very real to each band member. Barbara was performing for men her own age, many of whom were very badly injured.

One day the band played in a burn ward where sailors were recuperating after a recent accident on a navy ship, the Forrestal. The accident had been brutal. A plane had crashed on the deck, and burning jet fuel had spread everywhere. Many of these men had been seriously burned—not as a result of the actual accident—by their own heroic efforts to pull fellow crewmen out of the flames.

The letters we received spoke little of the horrors of the war, but mostly of the courage of the men. It was these letters that started us worrying a little more about the band's safety, and praying hard every night for their safe return.

An occasional package would arrive for Irlene and me with the letters. From every country they visited, Mom, Dad, and Barbara sent us a pair of dolls. Now, besides the letters, we had presents to look forward to. We missed our family, but we sure loved the dolls! Mom still proudly displays them in one of her guest rooms.

The next tour stop was in Vietnam. Suddenly the letters

Barbara and drummer Mark Peppard sightseeing in the Orient

quit coming. After receiving mail regularly for the first half of the trip, now we received nothing. Every day we would expect a letter but the mailbox would be empty. Soon we became very worried.

Irlene started to stare at the dolls we'd received. I knew what she was thinking, and in spite of all the encouraging words Uncle Al and Aunt Linda gave us, we couldn't help wondering what had happened.

The nightly TV news didn't help either. For some reason, even with all our worrying, we were drawn to those scenes of war. Those programs at least gave us a glimpse of where Barbara, Mom, and Dad were.

After a delay of over a week (it seemed like a year), several letters arrived together. They had been delayed for some reason. We never knew why. We eagerly read that the band was headquartering at a French-built villa in Saigon, the Majestic, and that the French food there was excellent. Still, from the minute their plane had landed in the country, they had known it was a place at war. (Daddy made Barbara wear a black headscarf when outside to cover her blonde hair and make her less conspicuous.)

The city was surrounded by sandbags and gun emplacements. At night they could see and hear mortar fire in the distance. During one of the first shows that they played, a bomb scare had forced them to stop and abandon their instruments until daylight. Another time a liquid nitro bomb was found outside their hotel, just six minutes before it was set to go off. The bomb was hidden in some souvenirs that had been confiscated from the Viet Cong.

Another of the early shows was interrupted when a group of paratroopers was called out for a special assignment. Since the men were not able to stay for the show, Barbara gave each one a kiss. That night some paratroopers were shot and killed before they reached the ground. We never learned for sure, but we believe those were the same fellows Barbara had kissed.

97

The band's performances were held mainly in the ballrooms of old hotels that were being used as barracks. The band did perform in the field, too.

The letters we received were not very descriptive. (Later, after the band returned, we heard the whole story.) The letters contained a particular note here and there on the war, but mainly spoke of the food, how big the rats were, and a particular car that Hertz had rented them. The car was a 1937 Citroën four-door sedan. It had to be push-started because of a weak battery, and it constantly stalled. Of course, it had no air conditioning and the weather was very hot. The windows had to be kept rolled up for fear of having grenades thrown through them. Dad couldn't wait for some basic American transportation. An army jeep would have been a limousine in comparison.

After two weeks in Vietnam, the band packed and boarded a plane to Taiwan. With all of them away from the war zone, Irlene and I slept better. The letters from Taiwan were decidedly more upbeat. They ate Mongolian barbecue their first night and later spent time buying hand-carved furniture and custom-made snakeskin shoes and boots. In addition to seeing the country they watched boxing, which featured kicking as well as hitting, saw lizards everywhere, and met the most awesome mosquitoes that they had ever encountered.

While in Taiwan the band traveled to one of their dates by a train pulled by a steam engine. There was no air conditioning, so all the windows were open. There were a large number of tunnels on the trip, and when they arrived at their destination, they all looked and smelled of smoke and ashes. (One look at the band and the audience must have expected a hot show!)

The servicemen had not had any entertainment from the United States in many months, so the audiences were both large and enthusiastic. The letters revealed that everybody was much more relaxed than they had been in Vietnam. They seemed to be having fun again.

From Taiwan the Mandrell Family Band journeyed to Thailand. This beautiful and historic country offered fascinating temples and monasteries, taxis that were three-wheeled bicycles, exquisite mahogany wood furniture and sculpture, tigers, cobra snakes, and elephants. Thailand is best remembered as the place where Barbara rode an elephant and Daddy turned down a chance to join a tiger hunt.

After a brief four-hour layover in Hong Kong, the next tour stop was South Korea. Even though not at war, Korea was still a country divided and explosive. There was an atmosphere of tension, much like Vietnam. By now the tour was winding down, and the traveling and the foreign food were starting to affect the travelers. Still the enthusiastic response of the troops and the special feeling that Barbara developed for the Korean street children made this stop quite rewarding.

Every day Barbara would buy candy and pass pieces out to the children outside the hotel. With each passing day there were more children. By the end of the two-week tour over twenty kids were Barbara's new friends. The children and Barbara taught each other songs. Even though neither Barbara nor the children ever understood each other's language, they came to know each other's hearts. Music was again the universal language.

In Korea my folks and Barbara also attended a church service that was conducted entirely in Korean. The men and women sat on opposite sides of the sanctuary, except for Mom, who sat with Dad. Except for the language the service was much like an American Protestant service. The hymns were set to the same familiar tunes, which reminded my family that home was not far away.

After crossing Liberty Bridge on several occasions and even watching a trained Army Canine Corps show (one of the dogs thought Barbara would make a good snack; fortunately it was on a leash and muzzled), the bags were packed for the final stop.

Guam is a small Pacific island that is almost totally military in nature. It offered a nice spot to rest comfortably and entertain American servicemen and their families one more time.

Many historic and meaningful flights have left Guam—presidents, generals, and other dignitaries had all flown off the island. Still no flight could have ever been as important to me as that August flight that brought my family safely home. The airport scene has completely faded from my memory, but I'll never forget the sight of Mom, Dad, and Barbara coming into view for the first time in thirteen weeks. My childlike faith had known that they would come back, but the proof was in the hugging. When I saw them I vowed to be on the next trip, if ever there was one. I wouldn't let music separate us again.

In just a matter of days after their return Barbara joined Ken at a naval base in Washington state, and Mom and Dad began packing up all of our belongings. My folks had decided to sell the businesses and our home in Oceanside and move to West Tennessee where one of Daddy's brothers lived. Daddy wanted to start a construction business, and since he had saved and invested his money wisely, the transition would be easy. Irlene and I, just happy to be with Mom and Dad, enthusiastically helped them pack and said good-by to all our friends. We looked forward to making new friends in Tennessee, and moving was much easier just knowing we were with our family again—this time to stay.

In Tennessee we would build a new house, go to my Uncle Ira's church, and I would get a chance to play junior-high basketball. It was all very exciting.

During the car trip to Tennessee we finally heard the stories that hadn't been written in the letters from Vietnam. As we listened Irlene and I were both a little terrified of what the band had been through but proud they had done it.

The Mandrell Family Band had been one of the first American groups on an independent tour to perform in the Mekong Delta area. While in the delta, late one night Mom and Barbara were being taxied by jeep to the showers just before bedtime when their driver decided to take them by a gun battery engaged in night firing. For security reasons lights on the whole base were off, and the driver inched the jeep along in almost pitch black. Suddenly, when they were near the guns, a blazing spotlight flooded the jeep, and a plane could be heard circling above. The driver exclaimed, "It's Puff the Magic Dragon!" and Barbara and Mom began to shake with fear. They had heard about "Puff," an American attack aircraft that in seconds could blanket an area the size of a football field with rockets and machine-gun fire. Barbara stood up, waved her arms, and pointed to her blonde hair while yelling, "Don't shoot! We're on *your* side. We're Americans, too!"

The message must have gotten through, because the flood light blinked out and the bathroom trip continued without further incident.

Two weeks after the band had played in that area and returned to Saigon by jeep, an American rock and roll band was ambushed and killed on the same stretch of road.

Many times while waiting for transportation, the band would set up temporary stages in the field and perform. These troops were stationed in areas that rarely saw entertainment, and they loved the opportunity to hear some music from home. One outfit even gave Dad the first American flag that had flown over their camp.

Everywhere they went Mom and Barbara were given insignias, patches, hats, and jackets representing the various branches and divisions they had played for.

A normal day consisted of playing two or three shows and visiting as may as five hospitals. It was hard work, but it was easy to do because the rewards could always be seen immediately in the faces of the men.

A typical night meant sleeping in a recreation room, on a stage, or in a tent. Once the band even slept in an operating room where there was still blood left from the previous day's emergency surgeries. There were always sentries posted, and they taught Barbara, Mom, Dad, and the boys how to shoot M-16's. Fortunately, this newly acquired skill was never tested.

The sounds of battle, usually single shot after single shot, could always be heard. The firing never seemed to stop.

Normal transportation for "the broads, the bags, and the band," as their pilots said, was by helicopter—the best air-craft because a helicopter could take off vertically and fly higher than normal sniper fire.

The audiences were unbelievable. No matter what the weather, the time of day, or what had happened before, the band—and especially the ladies—was treated like royalty. The response and appreciation shown made the lack of sleep, modern conveniences, and good food seem like minor problems.

There were many special, heart-tugging moments in Vietnam, most of them happening in field hospitals. Often Barbara was the first civilian woman to see many of the soldiers since they were injured. Many men had lost limbs or suffered scarring wounds, and how Barbara reacted could affect how they accepted themselves for the rest of their lives. Barbara han-dled the pressure well and treated each individual as a man of strength. She prayed that God would give her the courage and the right words for each case, and He always did.

In one field hospital, in a section reserved for individuals in serious condition, the band played just a few songs with acoustical instruments. Many of the men in this ward, a number of them near death, didn't even know a group was entertaining them. As the band was leaving after this show, a young black soldier motioned for a nurse. The nurse then called Barbara over, and the young man asked Barbara to sing "Danny Boy." Kneeling and holding his hand, with only Brian's guitar as accompaniment, she began. As she sang she repeatedly asked the Lord for help to make it through the song without breaking down.

When she sang the last word, in a voice barely audible, the young man murmured, "Thank you." With a "God bless you," Barbara left. Later a staff member told us that it was likely the young man would not live until morning.

That night, when all the shows were over and the pressure was finally off for another day, Barbara cried.

As I listened to my Mom tell that story, while we sped down the highway toward our new home in Tennessee, I cried, too.

Chapter
∽ 6 ∽
THIS LITTLE LIGHT

*C*alifornia and a childhood full of memories were behind us, and we were now a part of the "Great South." It might seem a bit unusual to move to Tennessee to "get out of the music business," but with Daddy going into the home construction trade, that is exactly what we were doing.

Tennessee was a new and exciting adventure for me, a place filled with first-time experiences. I joined the junior-high basketball team, went on my first hayride, and had my first date. (I also got my first kiss!) Daddy took me hunting, too. In many ways I may have seemed like a son since I always wanted to do everything he did. Daddy wasn't perfect, but I was convinced he was darn close.

We didn't spend much time in our new home before circumstances caused us to leave and head for Nashville, but the times we spent there were good ones. When I remember those months, it is gospel music I always think of first. And any thoughts of gospel music always pull my memory back to Illinois and a time before our move to Tennessee, and then ahead to the present and the many things that I can call mine. I believe that if the family had not moved to Tennessee we would not be doing what we're doing today.

Growing up in the Mandrell family meant growing up with the priorities of God, family, and music—in that order. This was not difficult to do, especially if you like to sing in church with your family, which we did.

I was named for my cousin Louise. She was a church pianist and primarily responsible for teaching Irlene and me a song that immediately, when we were quite young, became our favorite one—"This Little Light of Mine." Our previous favorite had been "Smokey the Bear," and it took quite a song to replace it. "Light" not only did that, but it moved us from singing just for the family to singing for a much larger audience in church. This song was soon followed by "If You're Happy and You Know It, Clap Your Hands," "Deep and Wide," and so forth.

Since childhood a lot of songs have come and gone. Those uncomplicated tunes are more than just memories, they are an important part of my life. They are old, dependable friends.

Without Gospel music my folks would not have met. On occasion my father would join his brother and sister-in-law, Ira and Marjorie, to sing gospel music, and he was with them when he met my mother at her home church.

Mary McGill was an active member of her brother Ralph's church in that rural Illinois area. Music had been one of her first loves, and church offered her a great deal of exposure to it. She was naturally excited to hear this Southern brand of gospel music. She was particularly interested in the young, good-looking bass player about whom everyone had already told her. She was supposed to be the official hostess for him, and after one look, she decided the two-week revival held a lot of possibilities.

The next two weeks were busy for my mother with school, work, and good gospel music. Somehow, there was also enough time for Irby and Mary to get to know each other. No one seems to remember if the revival sermons were filled with hellfire, but there certainly was some sparking going on between Miss McGill and Mr. Mandrell. Just three months later, the guest and the hostess were married.

Hairstyles have changed

Mom taught all of us girls music as we grew up. Barbara, of course, at a very young age learned a variety of music quickly and well. She knew the words and melodies to various church hymns long before she could read. But as much as she enjoyed singing, her musical debut was made without her voice.

When Barbara was barely five, Mom taught her a song on the twenty-four bass accordion. Barbara practiced hard but no one at church even knew that she was learning to play an instrument. The church music director, though, was not a bit surprised when Barbara volunteered to be a part of a Sunday morning service. He knew of her enthusiasm for music and was delighted. On that particular Sunday, after Barbara supposedly had left to go to children's church, everything appeared normal until an independent, curly-headed, blonde bundle of excitement marched back into the sanctuary, carrying an accordion almost as large as she.

Mom's face must have registered a great deal of shock. Before she could even ask my dad if he knew what was up, Barbara started playing. Mom's expression of shock quickly turned to a smile as Barbara enthusiastically and perfectly played "Gospel Boogie." The congregation loved it, Mom was justifiably proud, and Barbara took the hint and encored. Barbara's love affair with performing had begun.

Except for a Sunday school rendition of "This Little Light" at Uncle Ralph's church, Irlene and I had steered away from the spotlight. This quickly changed, though, when we moved to Tennessee. My Uncle Ira had a church there, and we soon realized that he wanted to involve two adolescent nieces in a number of church activities. We had always enjoyed church, but now we became active participants.

Irlene has never hesitated to voice her opinions when asked, something Uncle Ira found out the hard way. One Sunday morning he asked her how she liked church, and my little sister—knowing she had better be honest when speaking to a minister—replied: "It would be a whole lot better with a lot less preaching and a lot more singing."

Uncle Ira listened, and music, which had always been a vital part of his services, became even more important. It wasn't long before Irlene played her drums and I played my bass guitar and fiddle in church.

About this time Barbara's husband, Ken, was transferred overseas, and Barbara moved to Tennessee to live with us. We were happy to have her back, and though we all missed Ken, we were sure glad that his timing had added a fabulous steel player to our little group. Barbara didn't have to be drafted either; she wanted to play.

We were enjoying playing together so much that we decided to go back to where it all had started for a weekend of special music. So our family, along with Uncle Ira and Aunt Marjorie, made a trip to Illinois.

Irlene and I worked very hard preparing for the show, both on our music and our appearance. We wanted to look just right. After all, we knew what Mom had accomplished when our father had performed in that same church years before; we naturally assumed that destiny would touch us, too. In other words, we were looking forward to some blind dates!

With Barbara the band not only had a new dimension, but another opinion on what songs we should play. Ultimately the newer generation—Barbara, Irlene, and myself—let the older generation—Uncle Ira, Aunt Marjorie, and Dad—win out and we sang the old standards. We did spice them up a bit, though. As it turned out the audience response was fabulous from both the kids and the adults, and contrary to some rehearsal fears, everyone still recognized "I'll Fly Away" and "Life's Railway to Heaven" even with a "funky" fuzz tone on the steel guitar.

As is the way with all good things, the show ended much too quickly. And it was a big success, so much of a success that Irlene and I didn't need any help getting to know everyone, especially the boys. This had been our first real show, and we loved it! We now had a great desire to continue with music.

Some years later Barbara returned with her band, the Do-Rights, to raise money for a church organ and to help gather funds for college scholarships.

Gospel music was the main factor in uniting our family for that first performance in Illinois, but its influence didn't stop there. It has played a big role in all our lives.

Irlene has always been beautiful

There are many examples of this. During a period in Irlene's life when she was modeling and out of professional music, she still played her drums at her church. Her husband, Rick Boyer, was a professional bass player who toured the country with Eddie Rabbit; but when Rick was not on the road, he joined his wife every Sunday, playing bass for their church.

My husband, R.C. Bannon, was raised singing gospel music every night of the week. He often talks of his days growing up as the son of a Pentecostal preacher. Gospel music runs deeper in his soul than just about anyone I know. R.C. even credits a member of his church with giving him the incentive to make his living from music. A man named Conley Gant gave R.C. fifty cents for doing a special dedication song for him during a Sunday night service. Brother Gant didn't know it then, but a half dollar seemed like enormous wealth to a four-year-old. R.C. kept singing and kept dedicating.

Barbara's kids, Jaime and Matthew, obviously are growing up surrounded by music. Between the road, home, and church they have been exposed to all the sounds. Yet many of the songs they have learned are the same ones we did while growing up. Obviously this includes "This Little Light of Mine."

Barbara has never quit singing the songs of her childhood, but her heavy road schedule keeps her away from home so much that she doesn't get to sing in church very often. Still, more people hear her sing gospel music now than ever before. "He Set My Life to Music" is the title of her new gospel album. She insisted in her most recent recording contract that she have the opportunity to do this special project. With artists like B.J. Thomas, Dottie Rambo, the Blackwood Brothers, Andrae Crouch, and the Mt. Pisgah Methodist choir on the album, as well as all of us in the family, it is very special. I love that album and the statements about her faith my sister makes through it, but there was a moment some years before when she made an even more special public statement of her love for gospel music. When I think of that night I still feel chills. In February of 1980, the Barbara Mandrell Show played before packed houses and received rave reviews in the showroom of the Las Vegas Frontier Hotel. I had a break in my road schedule and stopped in to see my sister's show. I felt very proud of both the response Barbara received from the audience and her excellent performance. I have never seen her perform better.

In the course of the evening she did most of her hits, played several different instruments, and gave the audience a taste of the many types and styles of music she loves. Toward the end came a particularly meaningful and touching moment. With the lights low, the auditorium hushed, and accompanied only by a piano, she began singing the gospel classic, "His Eye Is on the Sparrow." Slowly and carefully she shaped that old song so that each word jumped alive. The impact of each phrase drove home until shivers ran up and down my back. The crowd was deathly quiet, and all eyes were on Barbara. The mood held for just a moment at the end of a verse and then Barbara changed the tempo, stepped up the beat, and her band helped turn that slow gospel song into a hand-clapping, foot-tapping sing-along.

The change went immediately from reverence to excitement. After three minutes of silence, there was now joyful singing. When Barbara "amened" the old standard hymn, you could have lighted the auditorium with smiles, and mine had to be the biggest and brightest of them all.

Some people were surprised that Barbara would do gospel music on the Vegas strip. It is something that's not normally done, but I sing gospel wherever I go, too. To both of us it is a necessary part of each performance. Still, there are people who ask why, and the answer is easy. We Mandrells grew up with gospel music. It has been a part of our lives in good and bad, happy and sad times. To us it is more than music, it is our friend. And we're proud to take our friends with us wherever we go.

As I left Barbara's show in Vegas that night, I thought

back on all the places I had been, all the gospel music I had done, and all the people I had come to know better through my contact with it. Still the most persistent thought in my mind that night was how much that gospel music had meant to me and to my family. Without it, all that happened afterward would have been different, and we probably wouldn't have been nearly as close.

*Growing up in the Mandrell family
meant growing up with
the priorities of God, family, and music—
in that order.*

*A drive to achieve new musical goals
stirred in my heart.*

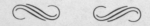

Chapter

~ 7 ~

FRÄULEIN

*O*n a special Saturday evening in 1968, Dad and Barbara decided to drive to Nashville to see the Grand Ole Opry for the first time. The experience was unique, entertaining, and somewhat magical. For Barbara the evening became more like a calling or the realizing of a mission in life. She left the Opry that night knowing that she had to get back into music. She no longer could be just a spectator; she had to be a participant.

Looking back now, that night at the Opry may have been the most important night in the lives of the Mandrells. The old Ryman was a building with a very special, infectious aura. When someone performed, the old walls of the building itself seemed to sing. Almost every foot of every person in the audience tapped out a drum beat on the old scuffed floors. Never before had Barbara and Dad fully realized the almost mesmerizing quality of country music and its artists, but there it was, all around that night.

All night long flashbulbs popped, hands clapped, and feet stomped. The people in this audience had not driven hundreds, and in some cases, thousands of miles just to hear country music. They had come because they lived and identified with the messages and stories of country music. These people were the real reasons why there was country music.

Perhaps the performers were only representatives—or instruments—that voiced the feelings and emotions of the individuals in the audience. The fans viewed these performers as people just like themselves. Hence mistakes or a lack of talent weren't values by which to judge them. The important quality was sincerity. To be a lasting success in this old hall, you had to sing and play with the most important instrument, your heart.

Barbara was never the same after that night. Halfway through the show she told Daddy, "I can't just sit here and watch; I have to get back on the other side of the microphone. I wasn't cut out to be an audience."

I think there was a gleam of satisfaction in Daddy's eyes when he heard Barbara's statement. "Are you sure?" he asked Barbara, knowing what her answer would be before he even asked.

"I have never been more sure of anything in my life. Will you manage me?"

My big sister didn't have to wait long for her answer.

Almost immediately Barbara went back to Nashville where she stayed with friends, Merle and Betty Travis and, later, Gordon and Virginia Terry. Barbara's first performance in Nashville was on the "Ralph Emery Show," which was an afternoon show. By the time the program was over, a couple of calls had come from "rip-off" record producers. But, again, friendship played a part in Barbara's career—Merle knew who the rip-off companies were.

Gordon was working at a club in Nashville's famous Printer's Alley, and one evening Barbara and Gordon's wife went to the club to hear him perform. Gordon asked Barbara to sing a number, and immediately the owner of the club wanted to hire Barbara as a featured act for two weeks. The deal was made, and Barbara was booked into the club.

By this time, the family had leased Mother Maybelle Carter's home and completed our move to Nashville. Barbara moved back in with us, and Daddy, naturally, attended her shows at the club. By the time of her last performance on Thursday night of the second week, Daddy had five business cards in his possession from record producers. One card was from Billy Sherrill of CBS Records. A meeting was set, a contract was signed, and Barbara's recording career was launched. Within months of seeing the Grand Ole Opry for the first time, Barbara cut a record in the music capital of the world.

When Barbara had been performing in California with the Mandrell Family Band she had made a record for a small label. With the move to Nashville came a record with a major label and a chance for national exposure.

On July 22, 1969, Columbia Records released Barbara's first single, "I've Been Loving You Too Long (To Stop Now)." It had been written and originally recorded by rhythm-and-blues great, Otis Redding. In early August I experienced one of my biggest thrills when I heard Barbara's new record played on WSM Radio in Nashville.

"I've Been Loving You Too Long" peaked at number fifty-six on the Top One Hundred charts, sixteen short of the magic Top Forty rating. Still, it was a very impressive debut.

Daddy had really put Barbara on the road and even booked her in a number of military clubs in Germany in early 1969. When she had returned with all the stories of her fabulous tour, Irlene and I decided we'd had enough. It was time for us to grab a spotlight of our own. Along with two girl friends from school, we put together an all-girl band. We practiced daily in our garage, and when we began to sound professional, we booked our first date at Ft. Campbell Army Base. Irlene and I had launched our careers—almost. Only weeks before our booking, the other two band members moved away leaving us holding the bag.

Daddy didn't believe in missing dates, so we kept practicing, and we also prayed for another set of band members by the middle of July. Irlene's drum and my bass didn't make for an exciting show—even when the girls playing them were sweet and a little cute. Cute got you a long way at a military base.

On July fourth a bottle rocket Barbara was holding exploded. She was treated for serious burns on her hand, and there was some question if she would recover well enough to play steel again. It was a time of great concern for us.

We shouldn't have worried about Barbara or our show, because on our initial date we were joined by our friends Joe and Rose Lee Maphis and guitarist Bob Wire and his wife. Needless to say, Barbara, bandaged hand and all, was there with her steel. Our first show was a smash!

The men at the airbase loved us, and Irlene and I decided that we would put together a new band and play more dates. We couldn't imagine anything that could thrill us more, but the best was yet to come.

Barbara had been surprised by how much her little sisters had improved on their instruments. She was very tired of working with house bands, but she couldn't afford hiring full-time musicians to back her up. Still, to have the caliber of show she wanted, she knew she must have her own band. Just maybe the necessary band members could be found in the Mandrell home.

On the weekend before her first single was to be released, Barbara had a booking in Vancouver, Canada, and she asked me to play bass for her. I was very excited and confident I could do it. So, on July 19, 1969, I played professionally for my sister for the first time.

The show actually seemed easy. My strong confidence was there because I could feel Barbara's honest faith in me. It was so much fun I felt guilty getting paid for doing it—well, not so guilty that I didn't take the money! My biggest reward came when Barbara said, "Louise, you did a great job. I am very proud of you, and I am going to see if Mom and Dad won't let me make you a permanent part of my show."

I was speechless, but I guess Barbara had said enough for

both of us . . . she usually does. My sister is quite talkative, and quite convincing. I believed her . . . and thought I had played well, too.

Barbara's next dates were in Texas, and she asked Irlene to join us, too. On the first evening Barbara knew that she had found the right mixture. Because of the consistency of sound backing her up, she was on the top of her mark. We felt her confidence and played over our heads. I got to do my first fiddle solo, "Black Mountain Rag," and I also received my first standing ovation. Irlene and I were now totally hooked on music.

Barbara convinced Mom and Dad to find private tutors to help us with our school work, and Irlene and I, along with Dad and one more musician, officially became Barbara's first backup band. We were on the road, doing what we felt we'd been born to do.

In many ways Irlene and I had reached the goal we'd set the summer when the others in the family had toured Vietnam. Then we had committed ourselves to becoming good enough musicians to travel with the family if ever the Mandrells got back into music. The years of practice had paid off!

A highlight of our initial travels was a chance occasionally to see Ken, Barbara's husband, when he received a leave. We genuinely were looking forward to his discharge from the navy so we wouldn't have to be content with short get-togethers. We wanted him back full-time.

Not long after one of Ken's summer visits in 1969, Barbara surprised us with some unexpected, but joyful news: "I'm pregnant!"

Suddenly knowing that Barbara was to have a baby, our biggest question became what to do about her career. Inroads were just being made with her records, and our group was booked for a large number of dates over the next few months. Decisions had to be made.

Barbara's expectant state seems like a minor problem now when I look back on it, but at the time it seemed pretty

Christmas before Barbara gave me my first nephew

major. After all, we had to consider the well-being of an entire family—including one member not yet born. The decisions made could affect the happiness of a new generation. A small child might make the pressures of the road worse, too. This last concern was a definite complication, and at first it tempered our elation.

After weeks of thought and prayer, Barbara ultimately decided that she could be a great mother and still continue her career. So nothing really changed, and we now started to contemplate the impending bundle of joy. If anything, we were all even happier.

Very few things have compared or will ever compare to the excitement I felt when I learned I was going to be an aunt. When Barbara said it was OK to spread the news, I told my friends, relatives, and anyone else who would listen about the upcoming event. Now the entire Mandrell family had a new spark in its life.

My folks beamed with thoughts of having a grandchild in the household, and even Irlene, who always seemed to take things in stride, got excited. It was a time when Irlene and I probably felt closer to Barbara than ever before in our lives. Now that we were a permanent part of her band and were on the road with her—and being exposed to all the varied experiences that go along with both—we had come to know her very well. We were a vital part of her team and now were more involved in this blessed event than we really had the right to be.

I became so engrossed in all the possibilities of becoming an aunt that I almost didn't notice that Barbara and Ken were equally as excited. I began planning as if I were the pregnant Mandrell daughter.

The whole family must have felt that way, too. Barbara was showered with attention, more than she had received in her entire life—from all sides of the family. Some of the attention, like being kept on a strict diet, I'm sure she could have done without. Still, we all meant well, and she was polite enough to put up with us. Actually, she may have just been making the best of the situation.

In some ways we were kind of mean to Barbara. Mom and I placed notes near food: "Watch your weight" or "Being pregnant is not an excuse to get fat." Barbara could not open the refrigerator without finding a warning. One time we came home and found the expectant mother with her head crammed into a cabinet door. When we turned her around we found an entire chocolate doughnut stuffed into her mouth—the entire doughnut in one bite! We let her swallow that one, but then we wrote more notes.

My excitement over becoming an aunt was temporarily interrupted about halfway through Barbara's term when, along with Irlene, I found out that we would tour Germany with Barbara in February and March. Not only would 1970 be the year of the baby, but also the year of our first overseas tour with Barbara.

My folks showed a lot of confidence in Barbara and our European promoter, Pop Phillips, even to let Irlene, who was then just fourteen, and me, only a year and a half older, go on such a trip without them. Daddy and "Pop" belonged to the same lodge so my mom and dad knew we would be well cared for. Also, by now Barbara had years of experience in looking after us. My folks thought of it as a maturing and character-building experience for us—and educational, too. So, with their blessings, we started to pack. I'm sure they said a few prayers and worried some, too.

Pop Phillips had previously booked Barbara in Germany and had become a close family friend. He was almost a secondary father figure to us. Because of Pop and all the friends and fans she had made on her previous tour, Barbara was eager to return to Germany. Besides, in her current pregnant state, I'm sure all those exotic German foods were very appealing. And overseas she wouldn't have to read all those notes in our kitchen!

Irlene and I were anxious and excited also. For us it was a chance to be on our own, a great reason to think of ourselves as more sophisticated, mature, and cultured. Hence, when we went shopping for a new tour wardrobe, we wanted the very latest in high fashion. Irlene and I loved the shopping spree Dad allowed us to go on. We tried on all the newest styles before deciding what looked just right.

Barbara had a more frustrating time shopping than we did. She has always wanted the right look at just the right moment, but when you are pregnant, the right look for the right moment is not always "high fashion." After many hours of searching and not finding, Barbara finally solved her problem by pulling out the sewing machine and asking Mom to make her clothes. Mom transformed the "in" styles into things for Barbara, not only making the outfits that Barbara loved, but those that flattered her. I'd thought before that being pregnant looked good on Barbara, but after seeing the clothes that Mom made, I decided it looked great!

Besides buying clothes there were other trip preparations, and some of them were not nearly as much fun as spending money. We rehearsed for days, and Irlene and I also packed and repacked a lot—long before our departure. We read and learned a great deal more than we had ever known about the world. Of course we also had to apply for passports.

I'd always thought of a passport as an exotic folder that was the epitome of romance and adventure. I think the movies had put this idea into my head. That glamorous vision of passports started to melt away when I realized you had to get shots to obtain one. It continued to melt when I found out you had to fill out forms that reminded me of school work. The glamour totally dissolved when I saw my passport picture. Passport pictures in the movies had never looked like this! At first I was paranoid that I might be turned away at customs. I knew that they wouldn't believe I was that ugly girl in the picture. My sisters and my folks assured me that the customs officials would recognize me and, that as a matter of fact, the passport picture looked just like me. If that were true, I didn't even want to leave the house, much less go to Germany!

When the big day of our departure finally arrived, we all faced it a little differently. Barbara was calm, assured, well-rested, and totally ready. Irlene was well-rested (as always), very eager, not too concerned about remembering everything, and behaving just as if it were another day. The other member of our party, guitarist Leon Bollinger, was looking forward to Germany but was probably a bit unsure about what a month overseas with us would really be like. Finally there was me. I was sleepy, anxious, excited, and very nervous about customs and my passport picture. I had thought the day would never get here, and now I didn't know if I wanted it to be here.

Waiting for the morning of our departure had seemed like a lifetime, but it went far too quickly once it arrived. Suddenly, I was awake, at the airport, listening to Mom's final instructions, and then in the air. As the hours of our rather uneventful flight passed, I put home out of mind and prepared myself for new experiences in a much older land. The small fear that had seeped in disappeared when I looked over at

Barbara. She was calm and assured. Seeing that, I stopped trying to look back, and with wide-eyed excitement looked out the windows and straight ahead, trying to imagine the adventure that lay ahead.

When we deplaned in Germany I suddenly realized it was time to haul out that awful passport. I also made the mistake of telling Leon why I dreaded this moment so much. Leon, who was quite a clown, then grabbed that small folder and proceeded to show it to anyone who would take a look. Embarrassed, a little mad, and very frantic, I chased him and demanded it back. By doing so, I created a monster. Now everyone in the immediate vicinity was interested in knowing just what it was that Leon held in his hand. Barbara, who liked to be very businesslike and serious in these situations, must have wondered what the remainder of the trip would be like. My sophistication and maturity had temporarily disappeared, but I rallied after we passed, without incident, through customs. I promptly hid my passport and hoped I wouldn't need it again until we went home.

Leon and I, and even Barbara, became immediately interested in our surroundings. Barbara pointed out buildings and other interesting sights that she had seen before. She also related what she remembered about the German culture and its people. Leon and I were very impressed, but Irlene was more interested in getting to the apartment and settling back into her routine—eating, sleeping, and watching TV.

As usual Irlene kept her unruffled perspective on life. Rather than "oohing" and "aahing" over all the routine sights between the airport and the apartment, she viewed it the same as normal life anywhere. Even at her age, with all the special attention she had received because of her looks and her being an entertainer, she didn't let any of it go to her head. She knew what she could do, and she did it. In return she only expected a normal response. As tired as Barbara, Leon, and I were, we could not calm down, unwind, and rest. Irlene was the opposite. She knew that she would see and learn a lot over the next month, so all she wanted was a bath and a bed.

Pop Phillips had rented for us a very nice three-bedroom apartment. After a quick inspection, we unpiled our gear from the van and set up house. Irlene and I had always shared a room, but Barbara asked me to share her room—that meant a lot to me then and now. Irlene took full advantage of this development and spent most of her spare time the next month sleeping in her private room!

Being pregnant, I guess Barbara wanted company, and since she was such a guiding force in my life, I was glad to be with her. That first night Barbara helped me settle in, but as the month rolled on, our roles reversed, and I spent a great deal of time taking care of her.

The next day we further arranged the apartment, and then it was time to set up on a stage.

The audience for our first show in Germany was made up of GIs and their families or their dates. This audience was typical of almost all others on the tour, and so was the location—a nondescript service club with tables, chairs, a stage, food, and wall-to-wall people.

We had only briefly rehearsed earlier in the day and were still a little unsettled. We had wanted more time to get ready, because a few important friends and allies, our personal instruments, had not been brought on the trip. We were not used to our rented instruments yet and were very nervous about using them. Finally, in a new country, with so many people in the club, Irlene, Leon, and I had a touch of opening-night jitters.

In retrospect, it may have been a mistake, but we had decided that Barbara was too pregnant to help us set up. We didn't want her lifting anything. Besides, she had a lot of fans who had come in that night, and we had talked her into spending time with them. The three of us, with some help from the folks at the club, set up the instruments and sound.

We considered ourselves very fortunate, because one of the

young men who helped us played saxophone. He put Barbara's sax together. Another assembled her steel guitar. Leon, Irlene, and I did the rest of the tuning, and all that we left for Barbara was the tuning of her steel.

When the lights went down and we moved onstage, my heart was pounding in my throat. My knees may have been just a little limp, but I wasn't very nervous, just excited. If I had known what was about to happen I probably would have been terrified. Introductions were made, the stage lights came up, and for a few moments we were a smash. Our instruments sounded great, and our flashy uniforms, white-and-purple slacks and jumpers, knocked them out. But that lasted for just a few moments.

The first sign that this was not to be a normal concert came soon after Barbara led off with her lightning-fast steel guitar solo. She sat at the steel on a stool that promptly collapsed. Still smiling, she caught herself, stood up, and played the pedal steel standing—at six months pregnant, no less. She did some unreal "licks," and I'm sure the stool incident would have been forgotten had nothing else happened.

We still had confidence! We still had the audience. After all, most of them had never seen girls playing instruments before. And we had a bunch of good stuff left. Smiling and assured, Barbara moved to banjo. She strummed her first chord and broke a string. It is difficult, if not impossible, to play three-finger, Scruggs-style banjo with only four strings on a five-string instrument. Somehow Barbara did it. She then looked back and gave us the high sign, assuring us with her expression that nothing else could possibly go wrong.

I'm sure Barbara's sax solo would have been more impressive had the reed not fallen off when she picked up the instrument. Smiling and mustering all the grace she could manage, she picked up the reed, tightened it, tuned the sax, and promptly blew the audience away.

When I noticed that sometime between my tuning and the show, someone had broken the bridge on my fiddle, I knew that there would be no fiddle solo because I couldn't play at all. Considering how things were going that was a blessing. If anything, I was relieved.

With the fiddle solo cancelled, Barbara moved into the singing part of the show. We breathed a sigh of relief when the microphone worked perfectly. Unfortunately the mikes for the backup singers were dead, and to harmonize, Leon and I had to stand on each side of Barbara, playing our guitars and sharing her mike. It was quite a sight—two short girls, one pregnant and one just big-eyed, and a six-foot, four-inch guitar player, all hunched around the same microphone. Barbara and I were on tiptoe to sing into the mike, and Leon was stooped. The sound mix throughout that club must have been unique.

We saw Pop Phillips in the back cheering us on. Evidently that meant he still had confidence in us and the rest of the act. It also meant that we had survived the first part of the show pretty well. But just as I began to feel good about the evening, I noticed the eyes in the crowd growing larger and larger. They were looking away from the stage. About then I noticed a strange smell, like electrical wiring burning. Looking back over my shoulder I noticed that my amplifier was smoking. I couldn't believe it. Evidently neither could anyone else. Leon began to edge away from that amp, but I just kept playing. The more I played, the more the amp smoked. The only thing my young mind could think of was: *I sure hope I don't have to pay for this*.

It must have been the loudest explosion in Germany since World War II when my amp blew up. In as calm a manner as I could muster, I unplugged my bass guitar from my now-totaled and smoking amp and plugged into Leon's amplifier. He didn't seem overjoyed to have me sharing his amp after seeing what my playing had done to mine!

Smiling, joking, and moving on, Barbara continued the show. Irlene had only drummed basic rhythms so far, but that changed when a leg fell off her bass drum. With the foot

127

pedal in the air, the drum decided to take a trip and proceeded to roll across the stage with my sister still close behind, attempting to play it. She finished the show stretching to reach that drum and playing high hat. Irlene didn't stretch like that again until she became a fitness nut in 1982!

I didn't know if we'd ever make it to the end of the show, and evidently Pop Phillips had doubts, too. During the last of our numbers I noticed his smiling face had disappeared from the auditorium. Wherever he had gone, I knew three girls and a guitar player who would loved to have been with him.

Finally the curtain closed, and Barbara, Irlene, and I ran for cover in the ladies' room. We hoped to regain some form of composure before returning to face the crowd and sign autographs. We also hoped that we wouldn't run into anyone who had seen the show. Too bad, but right in behind us came a lady who had seen the entire fiasco. She was crying with laughter and couldn't praise us enough. After getting our autographs she paused to ask me how long it had taken us to work out those humorous special effects.

Back at the apartment we slept well, knowing that the next day, with new and different instruments, just had to be better.

Thankfully, the next day was better but the following nights were not always so restful for Barbara or myself. As the tour went on Irlene and I attempted to take care of Barbara. We constantly fussed at her about working too hard, not lifting heavy things, eating the right foods, and getting enough rest. She got used to all the fussing, but she didn't always follow our advice. As a matter of fact she actually functioned quite normally. Onstage she was even better than normal; she was great!

After that disastrous first night the shows took on their old flair, and we took on a new confidence. The crowd response was great, and we made many new friends among both the Germans and the GIs.

Between the shows there was little time to do anything except pack up, pile in our van, and go to the next show. We usually did two or three shows a day, and when the last one was over, we were generally too tired to do anything but head back to the apartment and go to bed.

Heading to bed didn't always mean getting to sleep. Barbara was having problems with cramps, particularly in her legs. There were times when she woke up screaming from the pain. This scared me, and I didn't know what to do or say. I just massaged her legs and rambled on about things she had probably heard too many times before. I'd warn her again and again about working too hard and not getting enough of the right things to eat. She politely listened and agreed, just as long as I kept up my massage.

After the pain subsided, Barbara would trade roles with me and would start to take care of me. She would assure her little sister that everything was fine, and that she would make me a proud aunt. With the magic words *baby* and *aunt*, she relieved my fears and started my dreams anew.

For hours we talked about my niece or nephew who would be here in only two short months. We talked about the child's future, including everything from what kind of stroller he or she would need to whether or not we wanted him or her to one day be president of the United States. During that month of restless nights we must have planned and replanned that yet unborn kid's life a dozen times. Each time it was grander and better.

But planning at night was not all we did. When we could find a little time during the day, we shopped for things for the baby. There had not been a baby in our family since Irlene, and since she was only slightly younger, I had not known how much fun shopping for a new family addition could be. It sure didn't take me long to find out.

Irlene busily shopped for little things for her new ''niece.'' Meanwhile, I had a grand time picking things for my new ''nephew.'' Barbara was busy compromising our choices. Rather than going with blue or pink, we grudgingly agreed to yellow and white.

Irlene and I loved to go from store to store just to look, talk, and giggle. While Barbara found all of this interesting and an easy way to keep an eye on her little sisters, she always worked up an appetite walking around with us. Irlene and I were very picky and wanted plain American food, but our pregnant sister hungered for something a little more exotic. Barbara always won. Grumbling, we would follow her into the restaurant where she wanted to eat.

Inevitably the German food that she ordered for us was extremely tasty, and Irlene and I would have to admit that Barbara was right again. Soon, when Irlene had caught the spirit of trying new German delights, she felt we would be remiss if we didn't try some of their world-famous beer. Fortunately Barbara stayed in control of even that situation. Irlene got to taste some nonalcoholic beer. As far as we know, that's all she tried.

We loved our month in Germany, in spite of Barbara's pains, the rented instruments, and our inability to understand the language. The people were nice to us, and the country was indeed beautiful and dazzlingly clean. Still, when our last show was over and the instruments packed up for the final time, we were ready to go home. At our young ages, the only thing that could top a trip to Europe, making a living on our own, and shopping for things you couldn't buy in the States was finally getting to go home. Even after being spoiled by Pop Phillips, making so many new friends, and being so busy for so long, there was a lot to be said for doing nothing at home.

None of us believed going home would be a problem. We were very tired and the thought that someone would want to keep us from going to the United States never really entered our minds. The airline ticket agent asked the standard questions, and then asked some more questions that were not standard. Barbara was asked the one question that I'll never forget: "How far along are you in your pregnancy, ma'am?" The panic must have shown on Irlene's and my faces, but Barbara kept her cool and pretended to be very insulted that the ticket agent thought she was more than four months along. The ticket agent seemed convinced, but then Leon came up with his big black boot bag, quickly stepped beside Barbara, and addressed the agent: "I'm her doctor. Is there any problem here?" A few tense minutes followed as the ticket agent stared at Leon, laughed, and, after some more bargaining, let us board the first 747 to fly from Europe to the United States. After all those anxious moments at the airport, we really were ready for a calm ride home.

After twenty minutes of the flight, when we were about to settle into watching a movie and were enjoying the comforts of the 747, we headed into one of the worst storms that to this day, I've ever flown in. Even this huge airplane was buffeted, and a stewardess had problems just keeping her feet as she explained that the 747 was one of the safest and best-constructed planes ever manufactured. Just as she made that statement the movie screen she was holding in her right hand fell apart. Suddenly we all started to question her judgment on how safe the plane really was.

The plane did perform well in the storm, and once we hit clear skies, it was a routine flight. We slipped off our shoes, watched the movie, enjoyed the view, and munched on food. Still, even with all the new things to experience, several hours was a long flight if you wanted to get home as badly as we did.

The most patriotic thoughts of all for anyone who has been aboard are probably experienced upon seeing America again. No matter how beautiful the place visited, and no matter how wonderful the time spent, your heart beats faster just by touching home soil again.

After being overseas without Mom and Dad, I had begun to understand a little of how an American soldier must feel when stationed far away from home and family. I now knew personally why the Mandrell Family Band's Vietnam and Germany trips were so important. We were actually a piece of America, come to visit other Americans. I now understood better the sacrifices of Bob Hope and many others who travel far and give up much for our troops.

I came home a proud, flag-waving citizen. A very special trip had developed a special appreciation for my country. At this point in my life the world seemed to be out there waiting for me to win. My road map was a musical staff and some notes. I couldn't wait to see where music next would lead the Mandrells.

*"I can't just sit here and watch;
I have to get back
on the other side of the microphone.
I wasn't cut out to be an audience."*

*We were on the road,
doing what we felt we'd been born to do.*

*When the lights went down
and we moved onstage,
my heart was pounding in my throat.*

Chapter

~ 8 ~

KEEP ON SINGING

*O*n May 8, 1970, I became an aunt for the first time. Ironically my sister became a mother and my parents became grandparents on that same day!

Barbara had some difficulty delivering the baby, and seeing her in such pain had put me in a panic. Finally, she was forced to have a Caesarean section, and then everything was all right. My nephew was born and named Matthew.

I had been in such an excited state at the hospital that Barbara called me that evening to check on my condition. After speaking with her I reported to the others that mother, baby, and aunt were all doing fine.

It was a wonderful time. Barbara was a mother, and Ken, the daddy, was out of the service and home. We had a big house in Gallatin (near Nashville), and Mom, Dad, Irlene, and I lived upstairs with Barbara, Ken, and Matt downstairs. This was as close to "The Waltons" as you could get in 1970. Ideal as the layoff was, it didn't last long. By the first week in June we were back on the road again. This time we had a baby with us.

Initially, our transportation had been a station wagon which pulled a trailer loaded with our instruments. Then, because of the success of the German tour and other performances, it became apparent that we needed a different and more versatile mode of transportation. Into our lives came "The Old Bus."

The bus was a vast improvement over the station wagon, but it was showing its age. The old blue machine had passed through many hands and logged many miles before being parked at our home. Unfortunately The Old Bus spent much of the time parked because of mechanical failures.

Painted blue with stainless steel trim, The Old Bus was hardly pretty, but it did have a certain charm. We also felt a bit more "big time" touring in a bus. The bus was equipped with a kitchen-lounge area in the front. In the middle was a bunk room for us girls, and in the back was a small stateroom for Mom and Dad. We had a bathroom and storage closets. Our luxury item was a phone connecting the driver to the stateroom.

The Old Bus was our home on the road, and even though aged and plain, it represented a place where we had privacy, security, and the comfort of family. One of the first things ever hung on its old walls was a plaque that read, "The family that prays together—stays together." No kidding, every night we prayed that the bus would stay together for one more day! Ten years and three buses later, that plaque is still in Barbara's bus.

Kent Morrison, a young man from Texas, had become our new guitar player, and Barbara played steel, banjo, bass, guitar, and saxophone. Irlene was on drums, and I played bass and fiddle. In addition to driving the bus and managing the group, Daddy performed on guitar.

The fact that we girls played instruments was the most fascinating thing to our audiences. Our most frequent encore requests were for instrumental numbers, such as "Steel Guitar Rag," "Mama Don't 'Low," "Black Mountain Rag," "Orange Blossom Special," and "Columbus Stockade Blues." The old gospel standard, "Satisfied," was also a permanent feature of our show.

Ken, Barbara, and my nephew Matthew

A very important part of each show was Barbara's solos. She sang not only contemporary country tunes, but old country standards and blues. As the months rolled by, my sister's new releases on Columbia Records became a vital part of each show, too. Barbara's recordings were receiving a lot of radio airplay and were starting to chart well. "Show Me" had become a legitimate hit. "Do-Right-Woman, Do-Right-Man" had been a big-enough seller to give the band a new name. We were now known as "Barbara Mandrell and the Do-Rites."

That group name must have pleased Mom and Dad a great deal. "Doing right" had been the basic philosophy with which we had grown up, and now it was our official handle. The name continues to fit even today. Barbara's band is still made up of young men who show respect for each other and the public. We didn't know it at that time, but the name "Do-Rites" set a standard that still exists.

Our initial dates had been in clubs, and while we still worked a few from time to time, we were now mainly playing package shows at fairs and conventions. Working a

A fair date in 1970

package show gave us an opportunity to perform with a host of true country stars, such as Bill Anderson, Conway Twitty, Loretta Lynn, and Sonny James.

By performing on a bill with bigger stars we became better known—entertaining many people who had come to hear someone else, but who listened to us, too. The exposure was worth a fortune. We were putting together a solid following of fans.

Fan is a word often used in a derogatory manner by many people. To the Mandrells, fans were, and still are, some of our most valuable friends. Essentially, they are our employers. By purchasing tickets to see us, buying and requesting records, and telling other people about us, these wonderful people have allowed us to make a living playing music. Without their appreciation and encouragement we would be forced to do something else.

I really mean it when I say how wonderful the fans are. Initially our few early fans gave us the positive feedback that made the long days and nights of travel a great deal more rewarding. They started the applause and, in many cases, helped create the excitement.

As an entertainer you accept a certain loss of privacy and freedom, but that recognition is what you are striving for. If the fans don't care about the entertainer, the entertainer doesn't last long.

Being a musician is not an easy life. We found that out in a hurry. Being a country musician may mean as many as two hundred or more one-night stands a year, traveling all night for days in a row, giving up a normal routine of meals, TV, and get-togethers with friends on a regular basis. You work hard, and you know that work and sweat alone won't guarantee success or recognition. A successful musician is part gypsy, part minstrel, part artist. If all of that is in your blood, then you have a chance. I guess we Mandrells all have those qualities, because we always loved the road.

As we traveled to every part of the country, we settled into a lifestyle that seemed "normal" to us. Irlene and I studied as The Old Bus rolled down the highways. We had daily lessons in order to keep up with our school assignments. Education was very important, or at least my parents throught so.

Now with Matthew growing and becoming more active daily, it was enjoyable watching him learn to do new things. Even though Mom took care of him while we were onstage, we all helped with his "mothering" when we had the time. The daily contact and traveling in the close quarters of the bus had given me a special feeling toward my nephew. At age sixteen I became more like a mother than an aunt to Matthew. Barbara gave up some time with her son so that I could spend time with him, and I took full advantage of her generosity. Matt and I played on the bus and visited amusements at almost all the fairs we played. I would have loved having Matt as my sole responsibility, but the music called me every night.

139

Barbara, Matthew, and I on The Old Bus

Traveling cramped together in a home on wheels we all had specific and daily chores; otherwise, our lives would have been chaotic. We also had responsibilities for setting up and tearing down our instruments and stage equipment. In our spare time we played cards, listened to the radio, read, slept, and, naturally, practiced our music. We also worked up new ideas to improve our show. If one of us said or did something unexpected on stage one evening and it caused a good laugh, we worked it into the show. We always tried to keep the routine fresh for both us and our audience.

As busy as we girls were, Dad was even busier. In addition to taking care of all the business matters, Dad also drove the bus everywhere we went. There were times when he would finish one show, drive the bus eighteen hours, perform again, and then drive some more. There were many days when we looked more dead than alive, and the road was literally draining the life out of him. But at the time I was too young to really worry about his health.

Just keeping up with a grandson and a home on the road would have been enough for Mom, but she also made all our clothes and uniforms for on stage. She didn't get much rest either, but she seemed to never lose her patience or complain.

On the road we learned to pull our own weight, do our jobs, and sacrifice a few comforts for the good of the team. With Barbara's career now blooming we were playing better dates, so the things we were giving up didn't seem too consequential.

One of the most important dates we played in those days was the annual Fair Buyers' Convention. This was a meeting of most of the individuals who booked talent for upcoming fairs. The better you performed for these folks, the more jobs you could get and the more money you could earn.

In 1970 the convention was in Dallas, Texas, and we had a great substitute guitar player, Cliff Parker. To present a uniform look and to emphasize our professional showmanship, Barbara bought Daddy and Cliff new lavender shirts and white pants. These were supposed to match the outfits Mom had made for us girls. Barbara must have bought the pants on sale, because when the men emerged from the dressing room,

Irlene portraying "It"

141

Barbara and the Do-Rites, 1970

you could see right through their slacks. Not wanting quite that much national exposure, Cliff and Daddy changed back into their suits and the show went on.

We were "on" that night and received more booking offers than we could handle. Now we could make enough money to write the slacks off as a business expense.

Playing fairs gave us an opportunity to see the country. It also gave us an opportunity to meet many different people in some very different situations. One evening we were playing with a package show at a fair in Philadelphia. We were doing one of the lighter numbers, "Long Tall Texan," where our guitarist had the lead vocal and we girls did the harmony on "He rides from Texas to enforce the law." One person standing backstage, dressed in a blue western outfit with white piping (he looked like a movie star, but no one knew who he was), must have had a few too many drinks and decided he would enjoy being in the act, too. Without anyone's noticing he came onto the stage from the back and pretended to ride a horse back and forth in front of Irlene. Because the man was dressed in cowboy garb, the audience thought he was part of the show. Two uniformed policemen came on and escorted our impromptu celebrity off the stage, just as we sang "to enforce the law." The audience thought it was planned. As we had learned in Germany a few years before, the show never stops. That night the laughter didn't either, but we hadn't written this wrinkle into the act.

Besides fans the next largest contingent of people we met were tow truck drivers and mechanics. The Old Bus was always on the blink. In country music a "breakdown" is usually a hot instrumental number. However, many of our breakdowns were mechanical rather than musical.

One time between Marion and Cheyenne, Wyoming, we burned out a rear end and were forced to call for a tow into town. The first tow truck attempted to tow us without removing the rear end of the bus and jacking it up. The tow chain snapped, the bus whirled around, Dad set the air brakes, and we found ourselves facing the wrong way on the shoulder of the highway. Oncoming drivers could not figure out how we had gotten ourselves in that position. Irlene decided to confuse the people driving by us even more by combing her long blonde hair over her face and putting sunglasses on, like the character "It" on the old "Addams Family" television show. She then placed herself in the driver's seat, feet propped up on the dash, and acted as though she were talking on the bus phone. Seeing her almost caused several motorists to drive off the highway. Irlene could find humor even in disastrous situations.

Finally, another tow truck pulled us into Cheyenne. There we discovered that the nearest rear end for the bus was in Little Rock, Arkansas. The repair parts would have to be

Getting back to nature *Fiddling around on a fair date*

flown in, and the bus wouldn't be fixed in time to make our next date in Las Vegas. There were no airline flights out that day, and all the rental vehicles had been assigned to a large rodeo in the city that week. The only way to Vegas was by Greyhound bus, via Salt Lake City.

We arranged to rent drums in Vegas and packed all of our makeup, clothes, and miscellaneous items from our luggage into Irlene's drum cases. To keep our uniforms unwrinkled, we hung them in a clothes bag.

Matt was still very small and needed fresh milk quite often. We had no way to pack it, or to keep it cool on the Greyhound bus, so we took turns getting off at the bus stops to buy milk.

In Salt Lake we discovered that the bus line had left our uniforms a few stops back. Our poor guitar player had to wait in Salt Lake for the uniforms to catch up to make sure they were transferred to the bus going to Vegas.

As we rode on the bus we did what came naturally to us—entertained. We taught new songs to the passengers, played games, told jokes, and made a bunch of new friends. Except for the luggage and connection hassles, it turned out to be one of the most enjoyable trips we'd ever made. We also arrived in Vegas in time to keep our record of never being late or missing a show.

Later that week Daddy flew back to Cheyenne, picked up the bus, and drove it back to Vegas. After leaving Las Vegas the bus broke down again in the mountains. As luck would have it, a local disc jockey came by on his way home from Phoenix and drove most of the group back to Las Vegas. Daddy had to spend the day waiting for a wrecker, as there was only one in Las Vegas big enough to tow our bus. It was almost dark when the tow truck pulled up, and Daddy realized almost immediately that the driver was drunk. Dad said later that coming back through the mountains behind the wrecker was the wildest ride he had ever taken. (And would you believe that while waiting for Dad that night the rest of us watched a "Partridge Family" TV show where they were on a trip to Las Vegas and their bus broke down?!)

We seemed to spend the next few months constantly waiting for the bus rather than having the bus waiting for us. If

Barbara with the successor to The Old Bus

the engine was functioning properly, then the power plant would conk out, and we'd have no lights, no hot water, no heat, no comfort.

On one occasion we were running late, and all the power went off in the interior of the bus. Irlene, Barbara, and I had just washed our hair, and we had no way to dry it. And we had no time to eat out! Hungry, frustrated, and running behind schedule, we were forced to drive on with only the air vents to dry our hair and one small bag of potato chips to eat.

When we arrived at our date, we had a few minutes to spare. We were to perform after a dinner meeting, and our local contact asked if we would like to eat. Before anyone else could reply, Barbara politely told the man, "Thank you, but we had something on the bus." Irlene and I could have killed her. And we probably would have, but it was time to set up for the show. We felt that this was taking the idea of suffering for your art a little too far. Performing hungry was not in our job description. Grumbling got us nowhere, though, and the show went on.

As much as we would have loved to dump The Old Bus, we couldn't and by now we could all see Daddy's health slipping. We knew that we had to have a full-time driver, a new bus, or some time off. If we didn't get one of these, we were afraid we'd lose Daddy.

Eventually, Daddy put a new factory engine in the old bus and life got easier. It performed like a trojan and would outrun almost everything on the road.

Barbara's career was growing. Every day she was a little more popular, a little better-known by the disc jockeys, and more respected by her peers. We knew her road to stardom was a long one and would have peaks and valleys, but she was taking the right steps to reach her goals.

Barbara's growing popularity was affording us better and more frequent dates, and we were now working practically all the time.

When you entertain every night in a different place and spend days traveling from one state or city to another, the

An early Nashville publicity photo

days, weeks, and months run together. Each day might have a quality that is a little different, but they still seem routine. The auditoriums, fairgrounds, and grandstands all blend together, and time is no longer measured in normal seven-day weeks but in the length of the tour. For a traveling entertainer, the time of the next show, not the day of the week, is of greatest concern.

Even within the jumble of two years of touring, special memories of equally special events jump out of the maze and remain fresh and clear in my mind. One of these memories is of Paducah, Kentucky, where we were invited to participate in a telethon for Easter Seals Hospital. I was thrilled; it was my first chance to work with movie stars.

I had grown up watching "Davy Crockett" on TV, and another favorite television show of both Irlene's and mine was "The High Chaparal." In Paducah we worked with Fess Parker and Linda Cristal, the stars of those shows. In my mind these two were "real stars." Maybe for the first time I was genuinely star-struck.

The Easter Seals Hospital telethon lasted for a full twenty-four hours. We entertained, guests talked about the needs,

*Performing on country music's
most hallowed stage*

and pledges were called in. We all became very involved and
completely caught up in reaching the goal.

Slowly the money total grew as we continued to sing and
play. We didn't even stop to sleep. We had a goal to make,
and if we slept we might miss something. Fess Parker and
Linda Cristal worked hard hosting the show. Everyone did
their part.

As we entered the final hour of the telethon, a young girl,
afflicted with a crippling disease, was wheeled out. After
being introduced she played a beautiful piano solo. She pushed
her twisted frame to the limit, and showed everyone watching
just what the human spirit can accomplish.

None of the "stars" who appeared on the show held a
candle to that child. Most people probably watched the telethon for our entertainment, but it was that little girl who gave
them a real understanding and the desire to help make things
better in the future.

Watching that courageous girl, I learned the potential of
the human spirit and the strength of the human soul. I felt
very untalented and very lazy in comparison. I left Paducah
with a little girl as my new heroine.

The other experience that forever will be written in my memory and stored in my heart is our first appearance on the Grand Ole Opry in May 1971. The Opry was still in the old Ryman Auditorium, and for a teen-age girl it was an experience of a lifetime. Only a few years before, Barbara had made her decision to return to music right in that auditorium. And without knowing it, my career had really started because of that evening, too.

That hallowed hall had a magical effect on almost everyone who entered. The stage had embraced stars like Hank Williams, Maybelle Carter, Patsy Cline, and so many more. Their influence could literally be felt.

Backstage I met the legendary fiddle player who to many people is the definition of the Opry—Roy Acuff. I was deeply impressed. To me he was more than a man who played the fiddle; he was a living legend. His style, work, and career had contributed to all of entertainment. I felt his presence everywhere I walked at the Opry, and I still can't think of that stage without seeing his face. As we got ready and I walked around the plain and simple backstage of the Ryman, I retraced the footsteps of giants and backup musicians. It was like waiting in the womb before your birth into the real world. To be a part of real country music you had to perform on this stage; without the experience you were not a full-fledged member of the inner circle, a part of the family. If I sound reverent, it is because I am. And I especially was that night.

As we walked out on the stage of that historic shrine, we could not have been any more proud or humbled. There we were, looking out on an audience that really knew country music, looking at the people that country music is all about. The history of country music surrounded us, and I felt as though the spirit of all the old-timers joined us on stage that evening.

I walked on the stage of the Opry as a country musician; I left feeling like a part of country music.

Chapter
∾ 9 ∾

FOOLED BY A
FEELING

When we were touring in 1970 we met a handsome young man. Ronny, who had won a Loretta Lynn talent contest, had impressive musical ability, and we soon invited him to join our band.

Besides playing with the "Do-Rites," Ronny also lived with us in Madison when we weren't traveling. Irlene and I thought of him as the brother we'd never had. Ronny and I became the best of buddies, and our brother-sister relationship soon became more like that of a boyfriend and girl friend. We were constant companions.

I'd never had a real boyfriend before; I hadn't even dated very much. Working most weekends and being privately tutored through school had taken me out of normal dating situations. I just enjoyed being with someone close to my age. Ronny became the center of my attention, and there were really no other activities to get in the way.

Over the next few months I dreamed of romance, a wedding, and living happily ever after. I could also foresee being the perfect wife and having a child or two. I knew that all these dreams and wonderful feelings had to mean I was in love.

After all I had had no other romance to which to compare this one, and I felt so happy. I now realize that the simple things I've just described go along with your "first love" or a typical high-school crush. If being in an abnormal situation ever worked against me and my sound judgment, it was then. Inside I really was a blissfully naive little girl, but I seemed so mature for my age that no one realized that I wasn't all grown-up. I did look older, too, which is a polite way of saying I had a well-developed figure for a girl my age.

By the spring of 1971 Ronny and I had convinced everyone, including ourselves, that we were in love. We planned a fairy-tale wedding for June 16, when we would unite for better or worse. Two innocent, young people were ready to conquer the world and all its problems. At sixteen my visions were a bit romantic and very unrealistic, but I believed life went just the way it did in the movies.

Our church wedding was beautiful. My sisters were my maid and matron of honor, and Matthew was the ring bearer. I felt so beautiful in my dress, and I was so proud to be surrounded by my family. Our honeymoon was spent on the bus working shows in Florida. Ronny and I continued to work in the band during 1971 and maintained the same friendly relationship we'd had before our marriage. The bus didn't offer much privacy, nor was it a place where we really had to solve any problems by ourselves. I hadn't felt any of the grown-up pressures of the real world; I was with my family and was married. Everything was perfect.

By Christmas Ronny was tired of the road and was homesick for his family in Texas. So he and I decided to give up music. Leaving my family for the first time was very hard on me. I had real problems saying my good-bys, especially to my nephew, Matt. It was like losing a son to go away and leave him, and he cried even harder than I did. When I stepped off that old bus a big part of me either stayed there or died, because I felt very empty and alone.

Ronny and I moved to his home town in Texas, and our problems tagged closely behind. We finished building a new

*My wedding day and my
matron of honor*

home beside his parents' house. I stained all the woodwork
and helped with nearly all the finishing details. I even stepped
on a nail. Ronny's sister and brother lived just down the
street, and his grandparents also lived in the neighborhood.
All of them were extremely nice. Not only did they help
finish our house, but they also helped me learn to be more
domestic. This was really my first stab at being a housewife,
and all I knew were the real basics. I felt I learned well, and
before long the household chores were going smoothly.

Once we finished building our home, I found that I didn't
have much to occupy my daytime hours. We needed some
additional income, so I went to work in a jewelry store. I
loved being busy, so I also began working with the choir at
church. Between engraving jewelry and song-leading, my life
away from home became very hectic, but rewarding.

The weeks turned to months and then a year and, except for a
few letters and some phone calls, I rarely visited with my family.
I had seen them only briefly on a few occasions, and I missed
them deeply. I began to notice I wasn't communicating with anyone very much. Through no fault of anyone, I felt very alone.

The most profound difference in my life, which I could not

readily define, was the quietness. I really missed noise! I never really had known anything but noise and frantic activity. Now there were no new people with new voices, no new guitar licks, no frantic "Hurry! It's almost showtime," no moments filled with applause. Quietness and calm don't always mean peace of mind, which certainly was true for me.

I also felt very plain. Ronny didn't want me to wear make-up and I preferred very simple clothes. When I looked in the mirror, I didn't look pretty. I thought I looked a bit washed-out; actually I thought I *was* a bit washed-out.

The radio, and occasionally the television, offered me a chance to hear or see Barbara. Her career was jelling nicely, and I missed my big sister's words of encouragement and her understanding. Sometimes, I would almost cry when I heard her singing.

Ronny and I were still great buddies, but we were missing something as a couple. Neither of us knew just what it was, but an ingredient just wasn't there. Our relationship had no depth, and we couldn't even find the words to talk about it. We both had emotional needs that the other couldn't even see, much less meet. Our relationship hadn't changed, but with more time and maturity I realized what hadn't really ever been there.

When the Christmas season of 1973 rolled around, it had been over a year since I had seen my family. Ronny's family had been nice, but they couldn't fill the void I felt inside. The Mandrells were planning a family reunion in Nashville, and I not only wanted, but needed, to be there.

Materially the thing that I needed most for Christmas was clothing, and Ronny knew this. He may have preferred that I dress plainly and wear little or no make-up, but he could still see my wardrobe needed updating. So for Christmas he gave me money to buy clothes.

I thanked Ronny for the money, but I told him I needed to see my family more than I needed something new to wear. I asked him to let me go home for a visit. Ronny insisted I use the money for clothes. My begging and pleading went on throughout Christmas Day, but to no avail. He didn't want me to go.

I couldn't sleep Christmas night. My heart ached more than it ever had before. I missed my family too much to bear the thought of not seeing them for another six months, or maybe even a year. I really needed to feel their love and be in their home again.

I believe that Ronny at least sensed that what I needed and what was missing from my life was at my home in Nashville. I know he knew that I couldn't find it with him, and maybe because of that, he thought he had to keep me isolated and was scared of what I would rediscover at home.

The day after Christmas I made a decision: I was going to use the money to go to Nashville and visit my family. I had to visit my home and talk to someone who could help me found out why my life was so empty. Ronny disagreed, but he didn't stop me. I don't believe he could have.

During my visit I once again found some peace of mind. I wasn't satisfied with my life, but I now felt I could work out my problems. For a month Ronny and I were apart, and we both began to understand that caring about someone and loving someone are two very different things. We were actually better off apart. Still, I believed that we could salvage our marriage and work out our problems.

Barbara invited Ronny back into her band, and he returned to Nashville. He and I were glad to see each other, but the feelings were still not deep. It was like two old high-school steadies seeing each other at a reunion and realizing that they had nothing in common except the bond of their school years. Instead of school years, the bond between Ronny and me was music, but search as we might, we couldn't find anything else. Life wasn't as frustrating as it had been in Texas, but things still weren't right between us.

In February, 1973, Barbara and the ''Do-Rites,'' including Ronny, went to Vegas to work. I stayed home. Mom had just

Barbara in her rolling "home away from home" (Photo by Jim King, Courtesy of Augusta, Ga. Chronicle-Herald)

had a cancer operation, and I felt I needed to be with her. Mom was basically fine, but I wanted to help and I wanted to be needed.

Mom's being ill had scared me. She was my role model and still my best friend. I had never thought about losing her before. Just the realization that it could happen had made me want to be close to her. I wanted to give back something of what she had spent years giving me. I was growing up enough to understand a little of what love means.

In Vegas Ronny found someone who needed him. This young woman provided him the emotional depth that he needed. He fell in love with her and spent every spare moment with her. When the band got back from the tour, Irlene told me that Ronny had been seeing someone else. I wasn't prepared emotionally for the shock, and my pride and confidence were shattered. I had never hurt as much or felt as low.

In a matter of days I became a bundle of nerves. I visited the doctor, and he prescribed Valium to calm me down and help me get through the next few days. While still reeling from this experience, I was struck by yet another staggering blow.

My Uncle Ralph, the minister, had always been to me the ideal man of God. He stood for everything that I believed was important in life, the very things on which I based my spiritual faith. He was a strong man, yet a forgiving soul. If anyone had ever made the sacrifices to live a Christ-filled life, he had. Now, in the dark of night, when it seemed my entire world had already come crashing down, a voice on the phone told me that Uncle Ralph had passed away.

In the middle of the night I threw my clothes in my car and left Nashville and headed for Illinois. I was alone, and I knew

Barbara's father-in-law, Kenneth Dudney, watches while Matthew and his mom try out the new Christmas toys

that I needed my family. My emotions were frayed; my physical condition weak; and my faith in God, man, and myself, destroyed. Not only did I not have any answers, but I had also run out of questions.

Hours passed. Tired, distraught, and sleepy, I drove on, attempting to stay alert. The road was unfamiliar, and the darkness and lack of traffic made me unsure of my location. Finally, certain I was hopelessly lost, I muttered, "God, if you really exist, show me a sign."

Suddenly, a light flashed ahead of me down the road. It was probably just a distant headlight, but I began to believe just a little bit again. I still didn't know where I was, and I was by now very tired. Then I saw the lights of an almost-deserted twenty-four-hour truck stop, and I decided to stop.

The truck stop was no different than hundreds of others where we had stopped when I was touring with Barbara: gas pumps, asphalt, concrete blocks.

After going in I asked a waitress where I was; she looked at me like I was crazy. Another lady responded the same way. It was then that I noticed a rugged, tall, and muscular man with dark eyes staring at me, practically looking through me. I was terrified.

I quickly went into the restroom, hoping the man would leave. After killing several minutes, I came back out, but he was still there. I ordered a soft drink and drank it very slowly. He continued to stare, and I felt very alone and very weak.

At a moment in my life when I had no trust in men, when I had lost my pride because of a man, another man was sizing me up and staring me down. I finally finished my drink, got up from my chair, looked at the stranger and said: "I'm lost, and I'm alone. I just have to get back for my uncle's funeral."

Suddenly I realized that I had blurted out information that made me very vulnerable. I had admitted being alone and lost; I knew that I had set myself up for something unthinkable. Those dark eyes continued to stare. I wanted to catch my words—why had I said anything?

Irlene and I at Fan Fair

Suddenly those same eyes seemed softer, and just as suddenly a voice, gentle yet strong, spoke. "Young lady, you're on the right road, and if you just put your trust in the Lord, He'll take care of you." The stranger had turned out to be my friend.

With a new sense of knowing the way, I started out to my car. As I walked across the parking lot I had renewed faith in God and myself. I wanted to thank that stranger. I turned and retraced my steps. As I came near the window and looked in I noticed the man wasn't there. He must have already left, yet I couldn't believe he had vanished so quickly.

I suppose that the stranger with the dark eyes was just another truck driver, just another man who cared about people. Still, no one will ever convince me that he wasn't an angel—my angel. His words not only helped me through that drive (I did arrive safely without incident), but they continued to help me as I went through the next few days.

Uncle Ralph's funeral was attended by an enormous number of people. In his lifetime, he had returned everything he had received from the Lord back to Him, His people, and the church. He was loved by his congregation and respected by the entire community. I grieved over his death, but I knew his life had not been lived in vain.

A flood of thoughts ran through my mind as I stepped into

that church. I had learned and sung my first gospel song there. Barbara, Irlene, and I had performed together there for the first time. Every memory included Uncle Ralph. Now he was gone. Still, he had touched me.

As everyone does at some point I now knew the reality of death for the first time. I also realized how much I needed the Lord in my life. Without Him, life seemed futile. I now felt I must base my decisions on more than just whims. I needed to ask God to help me. In the midst of all my grief, I felt renewed. I was anxiously awaiting a new day.

A few days after I returned to Nashville, Ronny came back to visit me. He offered me a chance to return to him. My pride, which had been shattered when he had left me for another woman, returned; but I didn't. I now knew that we had married for friendship and not love. Just asking me to come back, he had returned to me an important part of myself. I knew that he was asking because he felt that this was the right thing to do. I thanked and hugged him, but we parted—just friends, something we probably should have stayed all along.

I was alone, with no goals, no plans, and no future. I had lost my hero, Uncle Ralph, I had lost my fairy-tale marriage, and I had lost the idea that I could be perfect. But even with all the pain, hurt, and embarrassment, I had become a stronger person. My head was high. I was convinced I was ready for tomorrow.

*I dreamed of romance,
a wedding,
and living happily ever after.*

*Quietness and calm
don't always mean peace of mind,
which certainly was
true for me.*

Chapter

∽ 10 ∽

THAT'S WHAT FRIENDS ARE FOR

*T*here are times when all of us have a problem going to sleep, when we can sometimes hear our heart's beating. For a moment, we are actually aware of that miraculous organ, pumping the blood to keep us alive. Yet, normally, we never consider the mechanics of the heart or the miracle of life.

My father was the pumping, beating, life-giving heart of the Mandrells. His energy, direction, foresight, and will kept us pushing and striving. Yet, because he was with us everyday, we often took him for granted.

I idolized my daddy. I didn't run to him with all my problems, nor was he my best friend—those were roles that Mom filled. I just knew he would do his best to protect me and keep me from harm. There are some people who felt his wrath when he was protecting one of his girls. I loved him for that, and for all the sacrifices he had made for *our* careers.

When Barbara bought her new bus in 1973, she hoped Daddy's failing health would improve, and it did. Still, the physical damage had probably already been done, and just because the new bus wasn't breaking down every night didn't mean Daddy wasn't overworking in other ways. There was always something that needed to be done.

Barbara's career kept moving. Her road show became one of the most popular fair attractions in the country, and by the mid-1970s she was doing magazine, newspaper, and radio interviews on an almost daily basis. A book on the history of the Grand Ole Opry, published in 1975, called her, in so many words, one of the trend-setters for future female vocalists. Now her singles and albums consistently hit at or near the top of the charts. "Midnight Oil," "Tonight My Baby's Coming Home," and "Show Me" were just three of the reasons she was now recognized and rewarded for all of her past work. She was a "new artist with a brand-new sound."

In 1975 Barbara also negotiated and signed a new contract with a new record label, ABC-Dot. This contract would prove to be a very important step for the future.

Television producers had also noted her success, and offers for guest spots on both national and syndicated shows came in. Indications were that Barbara's accelerating career would be the family's most important memory of the year.

In 1975 I was single, working with Stu Phillips as a fiddle player on the Opry, and living at home with Mom and Dad. With Barbara's heavy road schedule, Mom and I generally had the house to ourselves. At this stage of my life I needed a friend, and I was grateful for my time with Mom. Whether it was playing with Matt, talking, or playing cards, those days were comforting to me.

In March Barbara had a few days off, and we all had some time to spend together. Barbara had become very concerned about Daddy's health. He had seemed to be in a great deal of pain recently, yet always told her he was fine. We all decided he needed a checkup. We also knew that he wouldn't go to a doctor for it.

Finally, Barbara said that she would quit touring if he didn't have some tests run, so he consented. Daddy wasn't about to let Barbara turn her back on all that they had worked for. Barbara may not have played exactly fair, but she won.

Daddy checked into Baptist Hospital in Nashville, and the doctors immediately recognized that he was a very sick man. Testing indicated he had already suffered a number of heart attacks, including a severe one dating back some years.

Then we all realized that he must have had his first heart attack one morning three years before. That day we had all just sat down for a big Southern breakfast. Daddy became ill and stood up, wanting to leave the table so as not to disturb the rest of us. He headed for the bathroom, but only took three steps before falling flat on his face, knocking his teeth loose and smashing his nose, which caused blood to splatter all around him. We thought he was choking on a piece of food, and we started beating on his back while he was lying there on the floor. This was while I was married to Ronny. Ronny is six-feet-four and muscular, and he put all of his strength into literally knocking the life back into Dad that morning. It seemed like an eternity before Dad started to come around. We all feel Ronny was mainly responsible for saving Dad's life, and we're so thankful he was there.

As the doctors and staff prepared for Dad's heart surgery, it became quite evident that my father was not going to slow down, even if he was in a hospital bed. As sick as he was and in spite of his strong medication, he continued to make daily telephone calls to keep track of the business. He wanted to be totally aware of how Barbara's dates were going and if there were any problems. He also had many people coming to visit him—his room had so many chairs it looked like an auditorium. Probably realizing that they couldn't stop him, the doctors left instructions that Mr. Mandrell could do just about anything he wanted.

While Daddy was in good humor and attempting to act normal, the rest of us were more concerned. Barbara and Irlene wanted desperately to be in Nashville, but Daddy had told them to stay on the road. All of his brother and sisters had come into town, but Daddy joked that they had made a long trip for nothing. He insisted that all of this was no big deal, and in our modern age bypass surgery was just routine.

I knew that at least part of the reason for these jokes and "business as usual" was to protect us. Underneath, in thoughts he didn't expose to anyone else, Daddy knew he might die. He let a little of this emotion show when he gave Irlene, Barbara, and me each a Bible in which he had marked a special passage of Scripture: 1 Corinthians 13.

Dad is a very strong-willed individual and held true to this even in these circumstances. While Dad was waiting for his surgery, he observed other patients moaning in pain when brought back up to the Intensive Care Unit. He vowed to himself that he was not going to let anyone see him like that . . . no matter what. His room was always filled with laughter, and he was forever kidding with nurses, doctors, and visitors. He even made up signs and had us post them on his door. He made new ones each day, and before long these had become such a hit that the staff was making it a point to come to see what was written on the latest sign.

The day of Dad's surgery, March 27, Barbara was scheduled to leave for London, but she didn't want to go. This time Dad won out and reluctantly she left. When her plane landed in New York, the stewardess told Barbara she couldn't leave the plane to make a phone call. She was determined, though, not to leave the States without checking on Dad's condition. She not only made the call, but succeeded in getting through to the recovery room and talked to Dad's nurse who reassured her on Dad's progress. She was then able to leave for London with a much less heavy heart.

Dad woke up in the recovery room very determined and his old self. When they were able to remove the tubes from his nose and mouth, he asked the nurse if he would ever be able to play the piano. Not knowing him personally, but knowing that his name was Mandrell and he was in music, she replied, "Yes Sir, Mr. Mandrell, you'll be able to play beautifully in no time."

Dad replied, "Good, I have always wanted to play the piano." The nurse had to exit hurriedly to keep from laugh-

Daddy—he does it all

ing in a room filled with patients recovering from surgery. When they finally wheeled him back up to Intensive Care, he made true his vow and could be heard singing, "Back in the Saddle Again." In just fourteen days he was back on the road with Barbara, as robust as ever. No one would have guessed he had been sick. In my mind he became even more invincible.

With Daddy back touring, Mom and I were the only ones at home. Everything felt normal again. I was dating, working the Opry on weekends, and still trying to get my head on straight. Thankfully, Daddy's health was no longer a concern.

In July, 1975, less than a month after my twenty-first birthday and just six months after his first bypass surgery, Daddy had another heart attack. Barbara was returning to Nashville for a short break between dates, and while still 125 miles from home, Daddy started having severe chest pains. They sped with the bus straight to the hospital, for it was obvious that Daddy's condition was grave.

I was visiting a friend that evening, and when the phone rang I somehow knew what had happened. Before the phone was ever answered I said, "Daddy's had another heart attack;

Roy Rogers and Dad with Roy's favorite shotgun

I've got to get to the hospital.'' My premonition was right. I rushed to be with my family.

When I saw Daddy I could tell that his pain was much worse than the first time. I left his room worried, scared, and shaken. Daddy's mortality had now hit me squarely for the first time. He had suddenly become flesh and blood to me. My realization shocked me. I had just been through Mom's cancer operation, Dad's first bypass surgery, my Uncle Ralph's death, and my divorce. How could I possibly handle this too? In the future I would understand that every one of these ordeals had only served to make me stronger but, for the present, I was once again crushed.

I could see the concern and anguish in Barbara's face. Dad was Mr. Everything on her tour. He could fix anything and could take care of every problem. Still, I knew she could make it without Dad. It would be tough, but she would survive. And because of all Daddy's planning and work, her career would continue to grow.

Irlene was now living in Montana and touring with another band. She had left Barbara to expand her own career. As he had during the first surgery, Daddy gave Irlene orders to keep working. She was worried but I knew she would be all right.

Ultimately I knew I, too, would be fine. I loved Daddy and was very close to him, but I could make it. Still, even with my slow realization of all of this, my anxiety remained. Mother had always played an important role in our musical careers—teaching, playing bass in the Mandrell Family Band, making uniforms, babysitting, cleaning the bus, and running the office. She was always there to do whatever needed to be done. I was not only afraid of losing Daddy but feared that if we lost him we would almost surely lose her too, as far as our careers were concerned. We all were really close, and I didn't want things to change.

During this period of frustration I was at the Opry one night and was able to talk to Connie Smith—a great entertainer, friend, and wise Christian. She was very instrumental in helping me through this crisis. I'm so thankful to her, and she will always hold a special place in my heart.

Daddy was scheduled for another triple bypass heart operation on July 29. The doctors had discovered that, because he had healed too quickly after the initial surgery in March, his scar tissue had actually inhibited blood flow. The surgeons once again prayed and then operated. We once again waited.

After a few hours that seemed like days, it was over. The operation was a success, and Daddy was heard singing "Oh, Me, Oh, My, Miss Molly" to the head ICU nurse. Naturally, her name was Molly. He was obviously on his way to a full recovery.

A new medication was prescribed to slow down the healing process. Daddy would have to stay down for five full weeks, so he moved the office to his hospital room. He also entertained the staff in his spare time.

While still in the Intensive Care Unit, he informed one sweet young student nurse that he was using positive thinking to heal himself more quickly. She humored him by asking what he meant, and he asked her to look at his heart surgery scar. It was obviously recent and looked very wicked. Then he had her look at the scar on his leg where the doctors had taken veins during the surgery.

"Why, Mr. Mandrell, your leg has healed so quickly that the scar is already going away!" the young nurse exclaimed.

Daddy told her that he had done that with positive thinking, and that he was now turning his positive vibes toward healing his heart surgery scars. He told her that he planned to have them completely healed in a matter of days.

Soon almost every student nurse in the hospital had entered Dad's room to view the miracle. Finally, the head nurse came in to find out what all of the excitement was about. She quickly informed the students that Mr. Mandrell had been pulling their legs by showing them the scar from his first surgery. Daddy was happy—he had pulled a good one.

A steady stream of visitors came to see Daddy every day. He tied up the phone for hours and had the nurses at his beck and call. He was practically running the hospital, or so he thought.

Barbara, Irlene, and I smuggled dinners in after visiting hours, and we'd all sing together, too. We soon realized that the question was not whether Irby Mandrell would survive his hospital stay but whether Baptist Hospital would survive Irby Mandrell!

When Dad was released he went right back to work. He opened a new office in Nashville and turned a majority of the responsibility over to Mom. She more than took charge managing the office and helping handle Barbara's and my careers. The crisis was over. It was a wonderful feeling.

By late 1975, Barbara had charted her first hit, "Standing Room Only," on her new ABC label. That title could have been a description of her road shows. Also, the Academy of Country Music had named her the Most Promising Female Vocalist.

Although busier than ever with the family business, Daddy still found the time to visit heart patients at Baptist hospital

Lynn Anderson, Dolly Parton, and Barbara at the Country Music Hall of Fame, Nashville

and preach the skill of their surgeons. When the year ended, he had regained his health and things were back to normal again. I felt certain that life would be perfect from here on out.

Chapter

∽ *11* ∽

ON THE ROAD AGAIN

*A*fter my divorce I settled into a lifestyle much like that of any other nineteen-year-old girl. I lived at home, dated, did things with my family, and worked.

My first job was as a waitress. I was proud then, and I am still proud that I was a waitress. It is a demanding job that is service-oriented. I worked hard and tried hard to be the best waitress I possibly could be. This job, which kept me busy and around many people, made adjusting to single life a lot easier.

About this time, Barbara started talking about and planning for another baby and soon made the announcement we had all been waiting to hear. I wasn't able to share this pregnancy with her as much as the first, but we did get together when we had a chance and, in between visits, I tried to keep a close check on her via the phone. Barbara made a special effort to talk up the coming event to Matt and soon had him including a request for a baby sister in his bedtime prayers.

Barbara was touring in a new bus and things were much more comfortable than before. Mother was traveling with them and helping with Matt. One stop was in Phoenix, and some of Mother's relatives (sister and brother-in-law Wanda and Les plus their children and a new grandchild) came out to see the show. Mother insisted on baby-sitting for them that night so they could enjoy Barbara's performance. Mother, Matt, and baby stayed on the bus. Matt retired to his room and wasn't talking. Later after everyone had left and Barbara had come to tuck him in, he did not include the usual request in his prayer. Instead he wanted to know, "Why did Grandmother have to hold that baby?" We knew we were in trouble!

Barbara continued to get along well and worked until her doctor and close personal friend, Dr. Newton Lovvorn, made her stop traveling—at about eight months. The baby was scheduled for delivery via a C-section on February 23. Before Barbara checked into the hospital that night, she performed at the Grand Ole Opry. This was her way of not only sharing this moment with her relatives but also with all the people she loves so much.

I went to the hospital to be with her. I just can't stand to see Barbara in pain, and she had to keep reassuring me that she was okay. The next morning Barbara presented us with a beautiful baby girl named Jaime, and we could hardly wait to hold her—everyone, that is, except Matt. He completely ignored her. Barbara made sure he was included in all the excitement and, with a little help and a little coaching, soon had him holding his new sister. From this vantage point, it didn't take Jaime long to capture his heart just as she had ours.

Music was still a part of my life, and since I was surrounded by music at home, it probably was inevitable that I would return to performing. Barbara's song "Midnight Oil" had reached number one—her first time! Times were exciting at our house, and music was the reason.

It wasn't long until I, too, was back into music heart and soul. I was fortunate enough to be able to tour with Stu Phillips and then later with Merle Haggard as a featured performer. I was back doing what I loved to do—travel and play music.

My favorite niece, Jaime

Stu Phillips was such an influence in my life as he was the one who convinced me to go back on the road again. I was also working the Grand Ole Opry with him when I first met Gary Buck. He was a member of the Four Guys, a group that appeared regularly on the Opry. Gary was extremely handsome and divorced, and he had two school-age children. I fell immediately in love with his kids, Laurie and Gary, Jr.

Whenever Gary needed a baby-sitter, I was ready. Whenever Gary needed help with the kids, I was ready. Whenever the kids would call and wanted me to come over, I was ready. I felt needed, something I really required.

Marriage was a bad word to me at this time. I hadn't even given it a thought, but sometimes when you don't think about something, it can sneak up on you. Soon Gary had me thinking and talking about marriage.

Even though I was physically attracted to Gary, I communicated more with his kids. Gary and I had very little in common outside of music, being divorced, and a mutual love for little Gary and Laurie. Because of my need for love, and the fact that his children did love and need me, I convinced myself that I loved Gary.

If my first marriage had been based on friendship, my second marriage was based on need and physical attraction. I almost immediately learned that it is easier to show affection than real love. Our union survived with my playing mother to his children. For all practical purposes that was all. I knew I had been fooled again, but I was determined to make this marriage work. I was caring for two kids who genuinely loved and needed me. I lived my life through them. I was den mother, party giver, and softball player. My only other interest was music.

The Opry really has a family atmosphere, and Stu Phillips was a fabulous man. The combination of these two elements made me comfortable, and I gained experience and musical maturity that I never could have received anywhere else. After all, I was working with legends.

My musicianship was improving, as was my confidence, but my relationship with Gary was going nowhere. It seemed we had nothing in common. As a mother I was fulfilled, and as a musician I felt rewarded; but I knew our marriage was going downhill. I think Gary had been single too long to change his ways. This was not my first experience with this kind of situation. Still, I was too insulated and hard to be deeply hurt.

Now it became a matter of how long I could ignore the reality of my dismal marriage. How long could I pretend that everything was all right? How long could I close my eyes to what was happening to me?

I found myself avoiding my friends and family more and more. I didn't want them to know about my mistake. I didn't want to fail again.

People began to make comments that my blue eyes didn't sparkle the way that they always had. The life was gone; I was quieter, too. Suddenly the little girl who liked noise and excitement preferred spending time alone. I hurt so badly; yet I pretended not to notice.

I wondered where I had gone wrong. My marriages were

flops. I didn't have my life together at all. Meanwhile, my older sister had everything together. I never once resented Barbara for this, but I sure would have liked some of her magic for my life.

I convinced myself that things had to get better; I knew that they couldn't possibly get any worse. I kept thinking that for two years.

Gary and I needed to communicate, but because he constantly worked, we didn't have much time to try. When we did attempt to find a common bond, it almost always ended in tears, unnecessary words, and actions that caused both of us pain. This pain went more deeply than anyone would know, and I learned to trust no man and never to turn my back on anyone.

That pain lasted beyond the tears. Try as I might, I couldn't find a way to show and tell Gary the pain he was causing me. He found solace through other relationships. I finally admitted that I was in the middle of another disastrous marriage. I was hurt, untrusting, and bitter.

I now knew what I should have known all along: I had married out of my need to be needed. I had married into motherhood and succeeded, but I never really had been the friend Gary needed. And I knew that I had needs he would never see. Sadly, I realized the time had come to give up on my second marriage.

Still, divorce was a hard route for me to take again. Living a relationship like ours may have been a lie, but admitting that lie to the world was very difficult. Because I had been through one divorce, the pain of my present situation almost seemed better than the pain of another divorce. Ultimately there was only one choice. I asked for and was granted a divorce. Divorce and death evoke many of the same emotions. You want to hide from the truth and the pain. You also want to give up. Deep down inside there is this little voice that keeps saying, "Stay away from the real world. Play it safe." I really would have loved to play it safe. After all, my trust in

This shot taken about the time I was playing backup at the Opry

men was at a low point. My trust in women wasn't very high either. Divorce was a losing proposition, and I definitely felt like a loser. I literally was in mourning.

I tried to hide those truths from the real world. I dressed up, looked good, and acted happy. I loved to run into my "ex" when I was looking like a million. I guess I wanted him to see what he had lost. There was a satisfaction in this. It probably wasn't right to feel this way, but it made me feel better. I believe many recently divorced women go through this.

It was pretty easy to see that my life was not totally satisfying or very rewarding. I needed direction and stability. I also desperately still needed to be needed by someone.

Barbara released in late 1977 a hit single called "Woman to Woman," and that kind of talk is exactly what she and I had when my marriage broke up. Barbara gave me an answer to the needs that I recently felt. She told me that I *was* needed—by an audience. She wanted me to get up on my own and perform. She wanted Louise Mandrell to sing all by herself.

I had sung some in the past, but it was just a standard here and there. I would do it, but I preferred playing fiddle or bass. I didn't think I was good enough to be totally on my own. No one can imagine my fear of singing on my own. I would have rather crossed the Atlantic in a rowboat. I really looked upon myself as a backup singer and musician, because the spotlight was reserved for exceptional talents, like Barbara's.

Barbara kept after me. She was a cheerleader pushing me on and giving me confidence. Stu Phillips kept the pressure on, too. He told me to look beyond working just for him, to expand my horizons.

My parents wanted me to try it. Dad said that he could book dates for me in a matter of days. Mom was the reason I was in music, and she wanted me to "go for it." She wanted me to grow to my potential. Irlene even volunteered to help put a band together, and she promised to drum for me until I found someone else.

Finally, I told Daddy that I wanted to be a gospel singer. He was willing to back me, but first he asked me to make sure this was what I really wanted. I prayed, but I didn't receive an answer. Still I loved gospel music. Daddy understood and convinced me that I could still sing gospel music as part of a country show. I could even reach a wider audience in this way. I prayed again, and this time I felt better about going ahead.

With Barbara's cheering, my folks' and Stu's belief, and Irlene's offer, I committed myself to being a solo act. With Dad's help I started the Louise Mandrell Show.

In May 1977 Daddy booked an entire summer full of dates for me. Irlene and I put together a band. We rehearsed every day for three weeks, working hours in a row. We did almost all of this in my parents' garage, so the whole neighborhood had a preview of our show.

One of our bookers, Joy Fleenor, named my band the "Country Classics." We were ready for our first date—or as ready as we could be. We loaded into Joy and Dan Fleenor's crowded van and hit the road. Our transportation was a long way from a touring bus, but with the van we made our dates in 1977. I was on the road again.

Our first date was a theme park in Knoxville, Tennessee, and we were to play there for an entire week. If we were bad we would have to face many familiar faces all week long with no excuses. We needed to start out good and get better every night.

I had been a professional entertainer for half my life, and I knew all the risks involved in walking onstage. I knew that there are times entertainers think they are good, but the audience misses the whole show. I was aware that all the work, talent, and charm in the world mean nothing if you don't communicate with the crowd. I was scared.

As showtime neared I found it harder and harder to relax. I also began to feel sick, and I had a strong desire to be back behind Barbara playing bass. I suddenly didn't want to be on my own; I just wasn't strong enough by myself. Yet, here I was. Fear can do funny things to your perceptions. Suddenly, all those people in the crowd were my enemies. They had me outgunned and surrounded. I really wanted to retreat, but I couldn't.

This was not just make-or-break time for my career, it was make-or-break time for my life. I had to face up to it. I prayed. My prayer was simply, "Lord, give me the strength to perform and help me give the audience something that they'll think is special." I was still nervous, but confident. Barbara was not onstage with me, but I did have the same special band member whom she always had with her. I was ready to play and win.

The "Classics" were onstage; the crowd was ready. I walked out, grabbed the mike, and hit my first note. It wasn't so bad after all. The whole first show was solid, the audience was behind us, and we walked off knowing that we had succeeded. I had met my first goal by completing an entire show on my own. I knew that the audience was not an enemy.

During the next few months my confidence grew. The early nervousness about my abilities had been replaced with the normal excitement I felt just before every show. I knew I was pretty good, and I felt I was getting better.

Soon I found that we were making special friends and seeing familiar faces almost everywhere we went. This helped make the long days of that first year's touring much more satisfying and rewarding. I remembered the same stage in Barbara's career, except then I had been just a member of the band. Now it was all mine.

With "Midnight Angel," "Married, But Not to Each Other," and "Hold Me," 1977 was a landmark year for Barbara. The name Mandrell was becoming known far and wide in country music. Barbara did a large number of package shows with the fabulously popular Statler Brothers, and every day she became a more important figure in the music business.

Many of my audiences contained a large number of Barbara Mandrell's fans or people who had come to see Barbara's little sister. Newspaper stories, reviews, and commentaries comparing Barbara and me became very commonplace. This was quite a comparison, a polished entertainer and a novice just starting out!

Some individuals within the music business, concerned I would have a problem escaping from my big sister's shadow, wanted me to change my last name. They honestly didn't believe I would ever have an opportunity to be really judged on my own merit. I appreciated all their concern, but these caring people needed to realize that ultimately I would be judged on my own anyway. If I ever made a name for myself, I would have to be compared to the best—my sister! Besides, I was a Mandrell, and I was proud of all that name stood for. I knew that the final result would come down to work, talent, and a little luck—if I had luck, then nothing else would count. I kept the Mandrell name.

As we improved as a musical touring show, so did the caliber of the shows we worked. One evening we really made the big time and worked on the same bill as the Statler Brothers.

The Statler Brothers are four of the nicest, most caring individuals I have ever known, and their show is one of the best. To play before them was not only an honor and a fabulous opportunity for exposure, it was also a challenge. The Louise Mandrell Show would have to be good, because an audience awaiting the Statlers was ready for excellence.

My band members were nervous, and the timing of this opportunity just didn't seem right. Barbara had been ill and was in the hospital undergoing tests. My mind and my heart were focused on her, and I wanted to be by her side. There I at least could be taking care of Matt, now seven, and Jaime, who was just over a year old. My show didn't seem very important to me, but for my career's sake, it had to be.

I don't normally force my religious or political beliefs on my business associates or fans. While I think it's obvious how I do believe, the fans pay to see a show, not to hear my views. My band works for me under my rules, but they don't need to hear me preach. This night was different, though, and I asked them to join me in prayer before the show. We prayed and then we played. We left all our problems backstage, and when we walked off the stage an hour later, we knew we had given our best. That's how the rest of the year went.

My emotions were mixed at the end of 1977 because I had lost my drummer. Irlene married Rick Boyer on December 23 in a small ceremony at Barbara's house. I was happy that Irlene had found her man, but I knew I would miss playing with her. Nonetheless, she found me a great new drummer who also became a close friend, Greg Ewen.

So January 1978 found me growing again, both as an entertainer and as a person. I had goals; I enjoyed my work; and I felt needed. Originally my love of family had brought me into music. Now it was the music itself that kept me going and *growing*.

*I convinced myself
that things had to get better;
I knew that they
couldn't possibly get any worse.*

*Originally my love of family
had brought me into music.
Now it was the music itself
that kept me going and* growing.

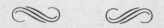

Chapter

∾ 12 ∾

ME AND MY R.C.

By 1978 my road show had progressed to the point that my band and I were traveling to our dates in a motor home. It was not a fancy motor home, but it was a step-up from the van. The new transportation made a statement: "Louise Mandrell believes she is going to stay in music for quite a while." I had taken a few tentative steps in 1977, but now I was ready to make a run at success.

A friend, Lucy Gray, came to me one day and volunteered to start a fan club for me. Lucy was a daughter of one of the original "Fruit Jar Drinkers," the first musical group on the Grand Ole Opry, and now I was thrilled that she would give up her time to help me.

A fan club can be an entertainer's most important organization, and mine certainly was and is. These wonderful fans are really friends with whom I keep in touch through monthly fan-club newsletters. Lucy also informs the fans of upcoming concerts and other important happenings. When I am on the road, these people make me feel that I have friends and family everywhere.

Barbara's mother-in-law, Beth Kurtz, headed up Barbara's fan club for years. There is no doubt that Barbara's success was due in no small part to Beth and her organization of thousands of fans. I was thrilled to now have Lucy doing that for me.

Besides the fan club, another indication that the outside world felt I was ready to climb the ladder of success came when Buddy Killen of Tree Productions asked me if I would like to record on Epic Records. I was more than ready to answer yes.

Cindy Duvall, a gospel singer, had been primarily responsible for getting Buddy to notice me. Buddy had recently offered her a chance at recording country music, but she had decided to stick with gospel. Yet, she did ask Buddy to take a look at my show. In Louisville, Kentucky, he caught my act, and then I received my chance.

I had taken part in recording sessions before, but never as the sole recording artist. I was both excited and nervous. Curly Putman, a legendary songwriter, had a part in writing the songs I was to record. Everything was almost too good to be true. On January 17, 1978, at Nashville's Sound Shop, I recorded for the first time. I felt good about the session. I was thankful that Buddy and Joe Casey of CBS had the faith in me to give me this chance.

About the same time Hal Durham of the Grand Ole Opry asked me to come back and perform there. That invitation meant as much to me as any I had ever received. In fact it meant so much to me that I turned it down! I didn't think I had worked hard enough or was good enough to deserve an Opry appearance. I told him that when I was ready, I would be more than honored to perform.

Barbara also recorded in Nashville in early 1978. She worked with producer Tom Collins and used material written by a new songwriting team, Kye Fleming and Dennis Morgan. She was very excited about her session and her career, too.

In the middle of the year, Barbara and I both released new records. Hers, "Sleeping Single in a Double Bed," became one of the three biggest singles released in the entire year.

A solo act

Mine, "Put It on Me," is now known only as the answer to the trivia question: "What was Louise Mandrell's first single?" Barbara was nearing the top, and I was near the bottom, slowly beginning my climb.

"Sleeping Single" was just one cut from Barbara's "Moods" album. The album was easily her best ever, and it became the benchmark recording that brought Barbara serious consideration from music buffs outside of country music. That album showed the huge scope of her vocal range and talents. I was very proud of that album and suddenly very aware of the great strides my sister had made in music.

Barbara's had become one of the most recognized voices and faces in the industry. In the past I'd watched her on syndicated country music shows. Now she sang on network music specials and made guest appearances in movies and in top shows like the "Rockford Files." Nearly every time I passed a newsstand in the grocery store I saw Barbara featured in a magazine article. Still, her popularity was most evident when we went out together in public.

I remember almost getting upset one evening because I couldn't talk to my own sister in a restaurant. Every time I would open my mouth or she would start to say something, someone would come up and ask Barbara for her autograph. I realized that night that if I was really going to have a conversation with Barbara it would have to be in private. In public she belonged to others. Times had changed.

As important as the "Moods" album was to my sister, "Put It on Me" was just as important to me. I now had a record label, a song to talk about onstage, and a special thrill of hearing my song on the radio. The sound of my own voice on the airwaves strengthened my resolve to continue working, and it was a beautiful reward for someone who hadn't even wanted to sing on stage a year before.

Ralph Emery helped make my dream of having a song on the radio come true. Probably country music's best known disc jockey, Ralph invited me to be on his WSM radio show before any other radio DJs even knew about my record. His interviews and plugs helped me up another step on the ladder to success.

After the fans, disc jockeys are the most important people in country music. They make the decision on what songs will be played, and their impact is enormous. If the DJs don't like you, your career is not destined for a long run.

Barbara was now working 150 to 200 dates a year, and I was working nearly that many myself. Almost every night meant two shows, autographs, a quick meal, and driving to another town. Still, the experience was a growing one, and the progress we were making was well worth the long hours and lack of sleep. More people were turning out for our shows, and the ovations were louder and longer.

As an individual I felt fulfilled again. I was doing something that I enjoyed. When off the road, I did some dating but was still somewhat guarded in my relationships with men. No matter how nice they were, I still protected my emotions and my heart. I couldn't take any more pain and didn't think I would ever want to marry again. I didn't think I could ever trust a man to honor a commitment. I still had some growing up to do in this area.

Annually, during the second week of June, Fan Fair is held in Nashville. Fan Fair is a country music celebration honoring the most important individuals in country music, the fans. Fan Fair 1978 was to be my first as a solo artist, and I was looking forward to both the work and the fun.

The week began with a softball tournament between the different celebrity teams, held on Monday and Tuesday. I played third base for Barbara's team, the Do-Rites. Barbara was our catcher. We didn't win the tournament, but we gave it our all.

I also spent some time at Barbara's fan club booth autographing pictures, and Epic Records had me autograph at their booth, too. I wasn't mobbed like Conway, Barbara, Dolly, and others, but I did meet some new people and talked to quite a few fans. (Chatting with fans is a luxury that I don't get often enough now. I miss it!)

In 1978 there were over twelve thousand fans at Fan Fair, and almost half of them would attend the CBS record label concert on Thursday. I was scheduled to sing a few songs there and was very excited about performing for many people who would be hearing me for the first time. The national fan exposure could be a big boost for my career.

During rehearsals for the show, I watched much like a star-struck fan as a variety of well-known performers worked out their numbers. One young singer-songwriter impressed me very much. He had recently written Ronnie Milsap's hit, "Only One Love in My Life," and he had scored very well with his own recording of "It Doesn't Matter Anymore." He was a very talented entertainer.

After he finished I walked over and complimented him on

his performance. He muttered his thanks and breezed out the door. As he walked off I thought, *How rude.* I shrugged my shoulders and pushed him from my thoughts. He needed a haircut anyway.

The CBS show was dynamite, and the crowd really seemed to like me. We ended the concert by having all the label artists come out one more time and sing a gospel tune together. Luck would have it that I was forced to stand beside that long-haired, rude songwriter—R.C. Bannon. Still, he could sing, and we both had been born in Texas.

An hour later fate had us together again, this time signing autographs at the CBS booth. I was nice to him, but cool. R.C. had to break the ice. "How are you doing? I really enjoyed your part of the show," he said.

"Thanks." I continued looking for a fan, any fan, who wanted an autograph. No one was around. The fans all seemed to be lined up waiting for Conway Twitty. I was forced to talk to this strange songwriter.

"Louise, a fan asked me to find out if you were married. He was really a nice guy, and good-looking, too—so I told him not to worry, I'd find out for him." Then R.C. smiled his crooked-lipped, Elvis-type smile.

I probably sounded a little sarcastic when I asked, "What fan?"

There was a moment or two of silence before R.C. smiled that Elvis smile again and said, "Me."

Well, there I was, left with two possible conclusions to draw from this conversation. The first was that this guy who had a crooked lip and needed a haircut was a little strange. The second was that he found out that I was Barbara's sister and wanted to go out with me for that reason. That can hurt your ego in a hurry. I couldn't really categorize Mr. Bannon. I left, actually not caring.

The next night I went on the late-night Ralph Emery radio show to plug my new record. After I finished, the "weird" songwriter was waiting for me, wanting to know if I'd like a

. . . but she caught it (Photo by Don Putnam)

ride home. I'll never know why I said yes. The last thing I wanted was to get involved with another musician.

We actually just got on the interstate and drove toward Kentucky. I decided I would have to scare this guy into believing I was a good girl so he would turn around and take me home. I talked about my faith, the Bible, and the Lord. I was sure he wouldn't try to kiss me if I told him about my religion. My tactic would get rid of this guy for good.

"I tell you, Louise, I sure am glad that I asked you out. We have a lot in common," R.C. said. "My daddy is a preacher, and I *really* grew up in the church. You know, we went every night of the week and a couple of times on Sunday. It is so good to talk to someone who can relate a little to that. I learned how to sing in church."

I knew I was in some kind of trouble then. Here I had brought up religion, and he knew more about the Bible than I did. Instead of turning him off, I had turned him on. What could I do next?

Ken and Barbara and songwriter John Bettis and fiance Denise at "Me and my R.C.'s" wedding

We turned around and headed back to Nashville at the Kentucky state line, and on the way back we ended up talking about music, our record label, and divorce. He had been through situations that were similar to mine. I found out during the next few hours of driving that I had a great deal in common with R.C. Bannon, and more importantly, I liked him. I scooted over closer to him, but he never did put his arm around me. Now I only hoped I hadn't blown my chance for a good-night kiss.

It was a great kiss, a great evening, and not once did the songwriter pitch a tune that was "just perfect" for my sister. I didn't believe, of course, that this could be somone special for me, but he was fun.

During my band's rehearsals a few days later, R.C. called me and asked where we were working next.

"Reno," I answered.

"Will you be going out via Kansas City or Oklahoma City?" he asked.

I thought for a second and answered, "Kansas City."

"OK, call me at the Holiday Inn when you come through. I have to be in Oklahoma City in three days, but I'll be working in Kansas City the night before you'll be coming through . . . so I'll just wait for you and buy you supper."

"Sounds great," I responded.

When we got to Oklahoma City I called the Holiday Inn. He wasn't there. He had stood me up. It was only when we got back on the road that I realized I had made the mistake. I sent him flowers to apologize. I honestly figured that if he did like me after my sermon, there was no way he would still like me after I stood him up by several hundred miles. I was wrong.

Over the next few months he showed up at a number of my shows, and he called every night. We had much in common, and new feelings started to come over me. R.C. and I had started out as just friends, but no man had ever made me feel the way he did. I forced my heart to be quiet; I wasn't going to fall in love. I just knew I'd get burned.

He talked marriage, and I told him it would be years before I could do that again. He talked marriage again, and I told him I would need at least two years to think about it. He talked marriage again, and I said, "Next summer."

Barbara must have suspected that I was deeply in love with R.C. When I discussed my plans with her, she approved wholeheartedly and offered nothing but encouragement.

Irlene was supportive, too. She told me, "You know, Louise, I think that this one might take." Irlene had the same faith as Barbara did, but as usual her way of expressing it was surely different!

CBS teamed R.C. and me as a duet in January of 1979, and we recorded "I Thought You'd Never Ask." R.C. did ask again, and on February 26 in Las Vegas, I tried marriage for the third time. This time I knew it was for better, not worse.

Barbara and Ken flew in to stand up for us at the wedding

Irlene and Tiger

chapel where we took our vows. R.C.'s songwriting buddy, John Bettis, proposed the only toast: "Two people, one love song." We watched Wayne Newton's Vegas show and then went to Disneyland for our honeymoon. My life was once again a fairy tale.

Irlene was on cloud nine, too, a totally devoted wife and preparing to be a devoted mother. My little sister was precious in her expectant state. She had always loved all of God's small creatures, but until now, raising puppies had been her main way of letting that special love show. Now she was going to have a baby. I knew that things couldn't be more nearly perfect. For the first time in a long while, all of the Mandrell sisters' lives were together and complete.

Then came the sad call. Irlene, almost six months pregenant, had miscarried. She took the loss very hard. I couldn't find words to really comfort her; I don't know that there were any.

When she returned from the hospital, she devoted more and more of her time to her dog, Tiger. Tiger was pregnant, too. When the puppies arrived they were small, white, and perfect. Suddenly they started dying. No matter what Irlene did, one after another, the puppies became sick and died. Soon there was only one left. Irlene was alone and in a state of panic.

Irlene took the puppy to the vet. He assured her that the puppy was fine. Relieved she returned home, only to have the puppy wriggle out of her hands and fall to the porch. When she picked the small creature up, it wasn't breathing. Irlene sank to the steps and cried. As she sobbed, she prayed: "Lord, I can't take any more death." Suddenly, the puppy moved, and within minutes it was back to normal. A small miracle, perhaps, but one my sister needed very much.

It took Irlene a while to regain her joking nature. She didn't want to go back into music, but she did want to do something. Just as R.C. and I released a song called "Reunited" and began our first Fan Fair together, Irlene tried modeling. She immediately landed several good jobs, her spirits improved, and she returned to being the happy youngest sister we had known for so long. For the brief time that she had been so serious, I had missed the girl who's always unpredictable and full of life.

R.C. and I bought a home next door to Barbara and Ken's in the fall of 1979, and it really seemed that the Mandrells were one big, happy family again. We all lived in the same town, we were all working on our individual careers, and we all had good marriages.

My personal life and my career were right on track. I felt good enough about myself to begin to worry about Barbara's career. I wanted her to win some much-deserved recognition for all her hard work. The time seemed right.

Chapter
∽ 13 ∽

REUNITED

If Irlene and I could be thankful for only one thing our folks did when we were growing up, it would be something that they *didn't* do—compare us to Barbara! They didn't try to make us be exactly like our older sister, either. The pressure to equal her talents, the skills she has obtained through effort and work, and a nearly limitless list of accomplishments, awards, and honors would have caused Irlene and me to quit before we even started. Fortunately, Mom and Dad allowed us to set our own limits, to develop our own personalities, and to find our own challenges. I never once heard, "Your older sister would have done this better."

For these reasons Barbara is more than a sister, she's a friend. She is someone to look up to, as an example of what a person can make of herself and of her life. She's not a threat, and to be truthful, I am as amazed by her as most of her fans are.

I doubt there are many people who work harder than Barbara. For starters, she gives practically every spare moment to her work—constantly striving to improve her skills, to learn new things, and to stay on top of what is happening in her field. She is a workaholic.

Barbara is also devoted to her family in the same way she's devoted to her music. She makes every effort to be a part of Matt's and Jaime's everyday life and still finds time to do special things for her husband, Ken. Most working wives who are that busy would use any opportunity to collapse or search for some quiet, but Barbara makes time for boating, skiing, and playing games with the family.

And if all the above activity weren't enough, Barbara never forgets Irlene and me either. She squeezes out time to spend with us. She wants to share both the fun times and the ones not so fun, too. Whether it's crying or shopping, she always seems to be there at just the right moment.

Barbara is not perfect, but she sure tries to be. She doesn't ever want to hear anyone say, ''You could have made it if you had worked just a little harder.'' If she doesn't reach one of her goals, it will be because something beyond her control stands in her way. She is not only the most talented and gifted person that I had ever known, but also the most resourceful, positive, and caring.

In 1978 she gave away another week of what little free time she had to support the Boys' and Girls' Ranch sponsored by the Alabama Sheriffs' Association. She put on a golf benefit and concert to raise money for the ranch and, during her week-long stay, became a buddy to almost every child staying there. Those kids practically became *her* kids, and she tried at least once to talk to each and everyone of them.

This first benefit for the ranch was held the week after the Country Music Association Awards in Nashville. Barbara had been nominated once again for Female Vocalist of the Year, and we all really thought that she would win, but she didn't. Barbara was disappointed but not demoralized or bitter over not winning. She was on top of her game while at the benefit, and the kids probably helped us all bounce back. Still, we naturally all felt that she had deserved that award—but there was always next year!

In 1979, Barbara once again was one of the final five nominees for top female vocalist. We all wondered if her moment had come. Naturally, the family all felt she had earned the award, but I was still concerned. I said some extra prayers for her!

The Sheriffs' Ranch Benefit that year was the week before the CMA awards, and all the work and fun we had in Alabama helped us not to think about the award show. This was R.C.'s and my first chance to golf as husband and wife, and the week was almost another honeymoon for us. The Statler Brothers performed at the benefit concert, and when it was all over, we had more than reached the money goal. The highlight of the entire week for me had come when Barbara asked me up onstage to sing a duet with her. It had been seven years since we'd performed together, and I was thrilled. We sang the old gospel standard, "Satisfied," and it was at this point I realized just how much I missed sharing a stage with my sister. I hoped we could do it again, but I knew the chances would be few.

On Monday night, October 8, 1979, I did some crying, because the Country Music Association named my big sister the Female Vocalist of the Year. I don't ever remember being happier or more relieved. Barbara's accomplishments had now been recognized and honored.

We didn't sleep much that evening. Barbara's band members, her record producer, and many others came by to share this wonderful moment with her. She had always made us feel that we were part of the team, and now we felt that the award was a little bit ours, too.

Barbara had always been a remarkable human being to me. Now, the whole world seemed to agree that she was special. If anything, I had grown even more amazed by her. Even with all of her success, she had not changed and was still a loving, caring, and sincere person. My heart almost burst with pride and joy.

The more people with whom I talked, the more I found out that everyone seemed happy over Barbara's award. I also learned that I wasn't the only one who knew of her special qualities. People who had never met her thought of her as their good friend, a result of her amazing ability to "have a visit" with every individual in audiences even as large as twenty thousand people. Everyone who ever had been around her seemed to carry a piece of her heart in their own. I loved this realization and I knew I didn't have to worry about my big sister's career anymore.

R.C. and I were soon back on the road, as was Barbara. Irlene had become the "Go Bananas" poster girl for Cover Girl Shoes, and Mom and Dad had just bought a new home. Life was busier than ever, yet we all seemed closer than we had in years. Life was a joy, and the problems (especially mine) of just a few years before were behind us.

When I had a break in my road schedule and was back home, I convinced Mom and Dad to go Christmas shopping and let me mind the office. All I really did was answer the phone, but one phone call led to one of the best Christmas presents I have ever received. The caller informed me that I was to work a network Christmas special with Barbara. Daddy had planned to surprise me with the news later, but I'm glad I didn't have to wait.

Soon after I got home, Barbara and I had a visit about the TV show, and she asked me what I wanted to sing. I answered, "It doesn't matter as long as I have the chance to sing with you." Just singing a duet on national TV with the person responsible for my singing career was enough—I wasn't too concerned with what the song was.

The timing for my appearance on this show was excellent. My career was at a point where the national exposure of television would be great, and this show would feature top names like the Gatlin Brothers, Ronnie Milsap, and the Statler Brothers. The ratings would probably be very good.

Rehearsals for the show started the same day that R.C. and I finished taping a series of commercials for the Internal Revenue Service in Los Angeles. The Christmas special was to be taped at the Grand Ole Opry, so I was forced to catch a "red-eye" flight from L.A. I arrived at the rehearsal in Nashville wearing jeans and a T-shirt that said, "If you're real good—when you die you'll go to Texas." Barbara who was dressed a bit more stylishly, took one look at me and said, "Nice outfit, Louise." Then she struggled to hold back her laughter. (I had the last laugh later when she made Mr. Blackwell's Worst-Dressed List!)

Later in the day Barbara and I sang through some of the old Christmas songs that we had sung since childhood. She had taught me many of those songs, and memories of a dozen Christmas Days of years past suddenly came to mind. I couldn't help it; I began to cry. I looked at Barbara, and she had tears in her eyes too. We both remembered how as children we had always performed together at Christmas. When Barbara had begun organizing the family Christmas concerts, Irlene and I had been too young to sing. We had just skipped around the Christmas tree or tapped sticks or clapped our hands while Barbara played a small chord organ. When we grew older we all sang together. In our childhood, Christmas had been complete only after our performance. Now, Christmas 1979 seemed more complete than any had seemed in a long time: We were performing together again.

As Barbara and I rehearsed I more fully understand how fortunate I was to have a family of so much love and togetherness. I felt very lucky and wished that more people could share the same blessings.

Barbara had Patsy Sled Vantrease, her dressmaker and close family friend, prepare a special dress for me. This immediately became my second favorite Christmas dress— right behind a red velvet one Daddy had bought me as a child. He had bought Irlene and Barbara dresses just like it, and we had looked "darling" for our Christmas program that year. I felt the same way now.

The show, the duet with Barbara, and Christmas were all

Me and my R.C.

over much too quickly. Never had I wanted to take a moment and hold it like I did the one when I sang with my sister. I'll never walk on the new Opry stage and not remember that evening—thinking about it still gives me chills.

After the Christmas special it was back to work. R.C. and I hit the road again, and my moments with Barbara were now few. Irlene and I did see each other occasionally when I was home, but it seemed most of the time we all went in different directions.

In early spring, the Academy of Country Music was to present its awards at a show in L.A. Barbara was nominated for top female vocalist, I was nominated for most promising female vocalist, and R.C. was nominated for most promising male vocalist. R.C. and I came to L.A. early to shoot an album cover with photographer Dick Zimmerman. Barbara had come in early too, and we all had a good time catching up on the winter's activities.

Before we were all together once more it was time for Fan Fair and the *Music City News* Cover Awards Show. These awards are important because the fans choose the winners. Without the fans we are nothing, so these awards mean a great deal to each entertainer and to the music industry as a whole.

Barbara and I were both to be on the show, but another of our family was to join us too! Irlene would be the model who handed out the awards. For the first time in years the Mandrell Sisters would be onstage together again.

Working the same show and sharing the same dressing room thrilled us all, even if we didn't perform together. But the biggest thrill was Barbara's winning the Female Artist award for the second year in a row.

Later that week we all signed autographs together at Fan Fair. None of us ever expected to work together as a musical act again, but being the "Mandrell Sisters" for a few hours was fun.

Barbara was already scheduled to cohost the "Mike Douglas Show" in July, and I was excited. This would be a new experience for her, but I knew she would do very well. After all, Barbara had had a gift for gab as long as I could remember! I wondered what "stars" she would interview.

A week or so before the taping, Daddy asked if Irlene and I would like to be on the "Mike Douglas Show," too. What's more the show's producers wanted the Mandrell Sisters to perform a musical number together. We couldn't wait!

When Irlene and I arrived in Los Angeles we were treated like big stars. We were given our own make-up artist and hair stylist, but we still had to buy our own clothes. We shopped

Barbara and I sharing a carol and a few memories

the day of the taping, and we found some very nice things at a price we could afford.

Our shopping trip almost caused us to be late for the show. We didn't have time to rehearse a new number, but it had been only eight years, what could we possibly have forgotten? The nearer to showtime that we got, the more nervous I became. But when the show began this feeling quickly changed to one of excitement and it just kept building as the show progressed until we were eventually reunited in our music—Barbara on steel, Irlene on drums, and me on fiddle.

The show was a smash—in my mind, anyway. Marty Krofft, a highly regarded television producer, asked Irlene and me out to eat as a result of our Mike Douglas appearance. Marty told us that he thought Barbara, Irlene and I were too good together not to be working that way all the time. We thanked him demurely, but told him our working-together days were now in the past. We each had our own career. Then he said some magic words, "How would you like to have your own network television show?"

204

Now this was an exciting and different matter. Visions of "Johnny Carson Show" guest shots and Emmy Awards flashed through my mind. It also seemed like such an easy way to make house payments. Suddenly, I came back down to earth. I gave him what turned out to be a short speech: "Irlene and I would love it, but Barbara won't. Barbara has turned down many network show offers in the past, and I know she won't want to do this one either. She is now a very hot item as a guest on TV, and her recordings and concerts are at a peak. In the past she has refused her own shows when they might have helped her career. Now she really doesn't need the help. There are no real reasons why she would take the show. I'm truly sorry."

Marty didn't miss a beat. He assured me that he could convince Barbara, but I left knowing he couldn't.

"Female Artist of the Year,"
Music City News Cover Awards
Show, 1979 (Photo by Hope
Powell)

Did you hear the one about . . .

Then, a couple of months after the Mike Douglas appearance, Barbara informed me that we were going to do a television special. If the public liked it, then we would do more. Marty Krofft would produce them.

I couldn't believe it! Marty had changed Barbara's mind—I would have to learn his secret.

Suddenly, Irlene's and my world changed drastically. We had to find places to live in Los Angeles, we did quite a few more radio, newspaper, magazine, and television interviews, and we worked on ideas that would lead to what forty million people would see on their television sets each week. But the biggest and best change was that we were working together again.

In September of 1980 I finished my road schedule, packed my bags, and boarded a plane bound for Los Angeles. My entire routine and lifestyle were changing. I said good-by to

R.C. (he would follow me out in three weeks) and left my home in Music City. I was more than a little overwhelmed.

The plane flight was my first chance to be still long enough to actually think about what the television show meant. I also got some insight into why Barbara might have changed her mind about doing a show.

Barbara had told me the show offered her an opportunity to reach a wider range of audience and was an opportunity for her to expand and grow, to be creative in a new medium. She also informed me that this contract was different from the earlier ones, in that she would have control over the final product. In other words, she knew the public would watch quality programming.

I knew that these reasons were sincere and true, but I felt there was more involved, too. I honestly believe that her two kid sisters were the two biggest reasons why she agreed to do the show.

For all of our lives Barbara had given Irlene and me chances to shine. She has always encouraged us to fully develop and use our talents and has been somewhere behind almost every success we've ever had. When she had deserved her own spotlight, she had included us. When she had received an honor, she had thanked us. Now, she was once again giving her sisters a special break.

As my plane flew west, I realized what a risk this show was for Barbara. If it bombed, her career could be damaged, maybe even ruined. She might have to work years to regain the heights that she presently enjoyed. If it succeeded, she would be the first female country artist to succeed with a network show, and she might gather a few more awards. But she might also become overexposed with her recording and stage business going flat. She was taking a big chance.

Once again Barbara was teaching me by example. She knew the show would help us—it was the chance of a lifetime. The world would have a chance to see Irlene and me as entertainers, not just as a famous performer's siblings. She was putting

In "Hee Haw's" cornfield with Mom and R.C.

into practice, "God first, family next, myself last." I just prayed I could find a way to thank her. I also promised myself to work harder than ever before.

Irlene and I had spent our first week in Los Angeles without Barbara. She was still in Nashville preparing for the Country Music Association Awards Show. This year, she was not only nominated but was also cohosting.

Irlene and I quickly found out that a weekly variety show was not all fun and games. We were subjected to daily exercise routines, acting lessons, and dance rehearsals. From the time we got up until we went to bed, we worked. Still the excitement of doing a television series made it all seem worthwhile . . . for a while, anyway.

Watching the CMA Awards Show on television was not like the thrill of being there, but when Barbara won the Entertainer of the Year Award, I still felt a rush of excitement. She cried, and I cried right along with her. I felt a little cheated at not being able to hug her and tell her how proud I was of her.

Several days later, to make up for our absence at the awards ceremony, Irlene and I greeted Barbara with a huge homemade banner at the airport when she flew out to join us. It read, "Barbara Mandrell, Entertainer of the Year."

Barbara had thought long and worked hard to develop ideas and concepts for the TV show. She and Dad had studied the successes and failures of other variety shows and had listened to many people tell how our show could be a step above those others. Upon arrival in California, the ideas were put into action. The show's final format represented much of that early preparation.

"Barbara Mandrell and the Mandrell Sisters" really did reflect our humor, talents, and beliefs. From the jokes to the gospel music, it was us. I later would say that the show was like watching home movies every week. That may be why it was so successful—that and a great deal of sweat.

Monday through Friday, and many times on weekends, we spent as few as eight, but usually ten to sixteen hours a day working on the show. Everyone had a part, and if you rested for an extra minute during taping, it might cost everyone an extra hour. One-hundred-hour weeks were not unusual.

We sisters had a great deal to learn. None of us were professional dancers, nor had we ever had extensive dance lessons. Now, we had to learn to dance well, and in just three weeks. When the lessons started I got sore in places I didn't know I had, but I did learn to dance.

We also had to polish our singing and instrumental skills. Barbara and I were used to singing the lead vocal parts, but now we would be doing a great deal of harmony work. We would also be singing a wider variety of songs. And instead of doing the same basic stage show every evening, each week we had to learn new songs and new routines.

For years we had been performing primarily as singers, still using our instruments on stage, but just as a sideline. We had to become complete musicians again.

People were provided to help us get our instrumental skills and bodies in the best shape ever. We also were constantly fitted for costumes and had to approve sets. Sleep became a fading memory—as did TV-viewing, spare time, and home-cooked meals. In recent years I had not had much time for those things, but now they were only dreamed-of luxuries.

Barbara continually tried to do too much. Long after exhaustion had claimed me, she was still at work, checking and rechecking various parts of the show. Big sister strived for perfection that even she had never reached before. As far as the show went, it paid off, but the toll on her health was too great. She became run-down and finally sick. But she refused to admit this and worked harder.

Our premiere show was on a Tuesday night with Dolly Parton and John Schneider as guests. Thankfully, our efforts were very well received, from the opening to the closing. The Krofft Puppets instantly gave us kid appeal, and the dancing and instruments fascinated a large part of the public previously not familiar with us. Reviews were on the whole very positive.

We girls and our husbands watched the initial show at Barbara's. We were quite proud, but also nervous about the size of audience we'd attracted. The ratings were great, and letters poured in. We were a part of a hit show on television.

NBC had been somewhat skeptical of the gospel segment of "Barbara Mandrell and the Mandrell Sisters," and Barbara had fought long and hard to make this the highlight of each show. She knew in her heart that the show wouldn't fully represent the Mandrells without a gospel segment. We were thrilled and grateful that the letters almost always mentioned that the gospel portion was the one enjoyed most. We were not surprised to learn that gospel music did have a place on sophisticated, prime-time television.

The second week our show was moved to what became our home night—Saturday. Kenny Rogers, an old family friend, was our guest. This was the first show we'd taped, but it aired second. The ratings were good again, and NBC decided to keep us around for the whole year.

Before long we were tagged "The Sweethearts of Saturday Night." With a parade of famous guests and old friends, we

*Even during rehearsals Barbara
entertains*

continued to do very well in the ratings. We made the NBC peacock proudly spread his feathers!

Dad had set up another office in Los Angeles where he was busier than ever handling any problems that came up on our TV show and taking care of all the contracts, letters, phone calls, and so forth funnelled to him from his Nashville office.

By now R.C. had arrived in LA and was enjoying just writing songs for a while, but Barbara ended his sabbatical in a hurry by making him the coordinator of all the music for every show. He soon was working harder than anyone, except Barbara. Every musical number went through his office. He picked out the opening songs, the gospel number, and duets to be sung with guests, and he mixed each song. He also had to satisfy all the guests. Songwriting became a former occupation for him.

Dancing can be work (NBC photo)

In many ways my favorite show that first season was our
Christmas episode. Our special guests were Mom and Dad,
and we all were together as a family. Daddy loved performing for forty million people, too. Mom would probably have
preferred watching.

We squeezed out a two-week break over the holidays, and
Barbara, Ken, their kids, and R.C. and I flew to Aspen to
spend some time together. Barbara lasted until Christmas,
and then she and Ken flew back to Los Angeles. Barbara had
worked too long and too hard on the show, and she checked
into the hospital, physically drained.

R.C. and I visited Barbara in the hospital when we returned to Los Angeles. One evening R.C. dressed up like
King Kong, and we waved to her from outside her window.
We wanted her to relax and laugh. We also hoped that now
she would become more conscious of her health and less
involved with every segment of the show.

We began taping again in early January, and Barbara was
back working as hard as ever. For the next thirteen weeks,
she all but killed herself. She pushed herself as hard as Daddy

212

had when he suffered his heart attack. I think we all feared the worst, but there was no way we could stop her. I knew that she felt horrible, but she still pushed on. During the taping of the season's last two shows, her throat was so sore it bled as she sang.

When we finally completed our first season and packed to move back to Nashville, we all felt like we had been through combat. The road and touring now looked much easier.

Before we left I filmed a commercial for national television use. I had become a spokesperson for White Rain Hair Spray, and on the commercial I played fiddle and talked about the merits of the product. (Yes, I do use White Rain!) This was a direct benefit to me from the network show.

R.C. and I had immediate business to take care of. We had mutually concluded our recording contracts with CBS and were now finishing up negotiations with RCA. Our first label had never found a consistent market niche for us, and we felt that a new label might better figure out just how to use us. RCA wanted to give us a try and thought our recording futures looked bright.

Very special TV show guest—June Carter Cash (NBC photos)

Ray Stephens making a guest appearance
(NBC photo)

Our exposure through the television show had brought us more work than we honestly knew what to do with. So we hit the road.

Our audiences were more enthusiastic than ever. The network TV show had jumped me years ahead in public recognition of where I had been just nine months before. All the hard work, those fourteen- and sixteen-hour days, were paying off.

In March of 1981, my home state of Texas made me the "Yellow Rose of Texas." Later, on May 26, Texas honored me with my own day. With Representative Neil T. "Buddy" Jones at my side, I played fiddle for the House of Representatives, spoke to the state Senate, and met in a press

Superstars, Donny Osmond and the late Marty Robbins
(NBC photo)

conference with the governor. It was quite an honor. Being recognized by my home state with the "Yellow Rose" and a day of my own was a dream come true. I couldn't see how life could get any better.

Two weeks later it seemed like Christmas in June as each of us sisters received awards at the *Music City News* Country Award Show. Barbara was named Female Vocalist and Instrumental Act of the Year. All three of us won Comedy Act and Favorite Television Show, and I was chosen Most Promising Female Vocalist. It was really too much to happen in just one night. We were truly being richly blessed, and I was simply overwhelmed.

Texas State Representative Neil T. "Buddy" Jones giving me my special day in Texas, May 26, 1981

The summer consisted of road shows for me and my R.C. We renamed our band "Spellbound," and worked at least twenty-seven days a month. Even considering the time and travel, this was easier than doing a variety show on TV. We at least could rest on the bus. The fan feedback was great, and in concert we could instantly evaluate ourselves. TV can't give you that.

Barbara continued to pull down awards everywhere, and she was also rolling up hit records. A live album had just been released, and her good health was returning. She was actually resting up as she worked the road! When I finally saw her in August she looked great again.

When September came, we all honestly dreaded going back to work on the TV show. We loved the final product the world saw on Saturday night, but we knew the tremendous price on Barbara's health. We knew she couldn't take many more eighty- to one-hundred-hour weeks.

To our pleasant surprise, our second season was easier in many ways than the first. We were given a week off for every three we worked. This was still hard on us health-wise, but a heap better than the year before. We also had the format down pat. The dancing was even a bit easier now that we had some experience and knew the left foot from the right!

A special development came about the beginning of the second season when the production company started looking for a little girl to play the part of Irlene growing up. Several people asked Barbara's five year old daughter Jaime to audition for the part, since she was the right age and actually looked like her aunt. The family was in there pitching too. We told her that she would get to dress up and look like Aunt Irlene on the show . . . that didn't convince her. We said that she would be on TV and her friends back home could see her . . . that didn't convince her. One of us happened to mention that she would get paid for it . . . that did the trick! She tried out and got the part. (The night she auditioned we were in "prerecord" with the Statlers. Kathy Brown, Jaime's governess, came in to give us the good news. Harold Reid's comment was, "Everybody that thought she wouldn't get the part, raise your hand!"

Jaime was perfect. She couldn't read the scripts but even this didn't cause a problem. The director simply read the script to her; she remembered her lines and came in on cue. Everyone was surprised that she was such a natural. I was proud of her but not surprised at her ability, after all I had grown up watching Barbara. Jaime and Matt's pictures were flashed on the screen each time we did the American Scene segment. Also, on the last show Matt and Jaime joined their Mother on the set while she sang "You Are So Beautiful To Me." I don't think anything could ever top that.

Toward the end of the second season the long hours and

Roy and Dale—"King of the Cowboys" and "Queen of the West"
(NBC photo)

draining work had taken their toll on Barbara. She had been going to a throat specialist, and he had advised her that nodes were growing on her vocal cords. This meant one of two things: She could either rest her voice or have surgery. Wanting a second opinion, we asked the network what specialist they would recommend. His diagnosis and recommendation were the same, and he told the network that she could not continue the show. NBC then released us from our contract. Barbara was able to get the rest she needed and this cleared up the problem of the vocal cords. By the time she went back on the road in July, she was the same great singer she had always been.

When that second season ended I felt pure relief. The hardest work I probably ever will do was behind me, but the payoffs would be worth the work. We were all now more successful because of the show.

On the show I had performed with some of the greatest entertainers in show business. Entertainers normally do not have the opportunity to see other entertainers work, yet I had gone one better: I had worked with some giants! In many cases I had made new and close friends, too.

There are segments of various shows that stand out as my favorites, and there are many entertainers who now mean much more to me. What woman wouldn't have enjoyed working with Patrick Duffy, Tom Jones, or Lee Majors? Who couldn't have fun with Phyllis Diller and the Statler Brothers? T.G. Sheppard and Mel Tillis was super, and of course, there were the likes of Ray Stevens, Conway Twitty, Johnny Cash, and Dottie West. My lifelong dream had been to sing with the "King of the Cowboys" and the "Queen of the West," and I did get to perform with Roy Rogers and Dale Evans. The list goes on, and it is awesome.

Still, even though the guests were great, R.C., Barbara, and Irlene were the most special. For two seasons, we were the Mandrell Sisters and worked as a team again. Every member of our family was involved, and the show really reflected us. When we finished our last taping, I would liked to have hung on to the family feeling for just a bit longer, but it will always be there—in my memory and on videotape.

Meanwhile, R.C. and I had released a new song, "Where There's Smoke, There's Fire." Our "Me and My R.C." album was selling well, too, and the state of Tennessee had just named me its official "Sweetheart." With the TV show completed we had two months to record a new album, take a vacation with Barbara and Ken, and put together a new road show. We did them all!

The spring of 1982 also offered two very special events. The first was the decade-old dream, a dream I was now fully ready to make come true. Hal Durham and the Grand Ole Opry asked me and my band to perform. This time I jumped at the chance. For a few minutes on that Saturday night I became a part of country music in the most special way you can, front-and-center stage at the Opry. My world stopped turning, and my soul filled with emotion. The audience re-

"Miss Country Sunshine," Dottie West (NBC photo)

warded my performance with a standing ovation, and I encored with "Orange Blossom Special."

A second special moment came later that spring at the same location, the Opry House. The *Music City News* Cover Awards Show, which had been so good to us the year before, asked me to be their cohost. Barbara had hosted this show before, as well as the CMA Show the last two years. In both of those years she had won "Entertainer of the Year." Now, I had an opportunity to undertake the same type of challenge. Our TV show had helped prepare me for the challenge.

The Statler Brothers and Ed Bruce hosted with me, Barbara performed, and R.C. was a presenter. Barbara won two awards that night, and we girls received an additional two awards. Yet, even with all of these reasons for this night to be special, none compared to a gift I was finally able to give my older sister. R.C. and I had written the words to the song

Fiddling on the TV show (NBC photo)

"She Believes in Me," and I was allowed to sing it as a solo. The song was now my tribute to my favorite and my personal choice for the greatest entertainer of all time, Barbara Mandrell. I cried as I sang it, and Barbara cried as she heard it. Never had a song meant as much to me, but there had never been a person who had given as much to me. I wanted the world to know how I felt about Barbara. The song was my public thank-you. I ended the song by saying, "I love you, Barbara." Had there ever been any doubt?

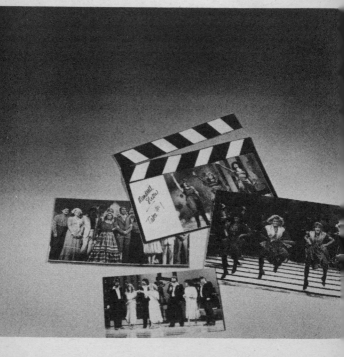

Chapter

∾ 14 ∾

REACH JUST A LITTLE BIT HIGHER

*F*an Fair 1982 was busier than any had been before. We were all very much involved in one another's careers, and we were also all going different directions at the same time—Barbara doing a label show one day and R.C. and I doing one, another. There were old friends to see, and hundreds of new fan club members to meet. There were very few quiet moments.

When I was blessed with a few minutes to rest, my mind continually drifted back to the late 1970s, when Barbara's career had really taken off. Much had happened and changed in the short years since that time.

I think it must have been because I was starting my own solo career during this period that, for a short while, I failed to notice that my older sister's lifestyle was beginning to change—and not by choice. When we had a rare opportunity to go shopping together, I noticed that many people immediately recognized her and wanted to spend time with her. It suddenly hit me—even when Barbara wasn't working, she still belonged to her public. She was by definition a "star." Because of this, people looked at her and reacted differently than they had when she had first started entertaining.

Signing autographs at Fan Fair

The success that she had worked so hard to attain now, in a way, had robbed her of a private life. At PTA meetings, in the post office, or even on a ski slope, she was still a celebrity. In some circles, she had been idolized—placed on a shelf reserved for special people. Barbara adapted well to this treatment. She still thought of herself as a normal person doing a job, and she must have wanted the real world to look at her in that way too. And what a job she was doing!

While Barbara continued to think of herself as just another successful working woman, her free time was being eaten up in larger and larger gulps. Everyone seemed to want to put a claim on her. The demands of concerts, television appearances, recording sessions, and interviews caused her to sacrifice hours of sleep just to juggle her career and her family. I sincerely wished that I could give her some of my spare time for her own use!

Watching Barbara I realized that I had never placed a high enough value on time. As her leisure time disappeared, I was able to see how precious are the little things in life. I promised myself that, no matter how busy I got, I would take out thirty minutes every day just to do something I wanted to do. It might be watching "Andy Griffith" reruns on TV, reading a book, making a cake, or walking, but it would have to be something that had nothing to do with my career. I was able to keep that promise for a long time, and these moments brought the peace I needed in my hectic, noisy world.

I knew that Barbara had to be tired, but her enthusiasm and energy levels onstage, in interviews, and on records were higher than ever. She may have not been well-rested, but she overwhelmed her critics, her fans, and her sister with her vitality. Her physical and spiritual beauty seemed to be drawn from her audiences. She must have been driven by her sense of responsibility to the fans who had helped bring success. At the same time I believed that, in the near future, Barbara's pace would slow down enough that she would be able to rest at the end of that year.

Five years later, I realize that the pace and the demands are still accelerating. I know now that she will actually continue working until she drops. I've seen her do it, and then get right out of bed to work some more. Daddy can't even get her to slow down.

Still, I wish that Barbara could have time to enjoy being the star that she has become, all the awards that she has won, and all the successes she has gained. But the bigger you are, the harder you work, and the pressures to touch all the people who reach out to you grow larger and larger.

Those same pressures seemed to be haunting me in 1982. I had less time to spend visiting with friends at Fan Fair than ever before. I kept thinking that things would slow down, but they never did. At the end of the week, I was totally worn out.

Barbara, Ken and the kids at
Disney World

The week after Fan Fair I got use to my "celebrity" status to sponsor a Paducah, Kentucky, golf tournament to benefit the Easter Seal Society. This was my second year involved with the tournament, and the whole event, including dinners, my concert, and my education concerning the work of the society, were exactly the things I needed at this point in my life. The unhurried pace gave me a chance to relax and get to know people. I also had a chance to play a little golf and, in the process, notice things like blue skies, green grass, and my own laugh. I loved performing, but the tournament gave me a week to spend a little time at a normal pace and in a normal world. But I was more impressed with seeing people take time out from their busy occupations to help other human beings. These are the kinds of people who make up a part of every audience for whom I perform. It was good to get to know them in this manner.

Somewhere in the back of my mind I realized that my career had begun to really take off. My latest single, "You Sure Know Your Way Around My Heart," had done better on the charts than anything I had previously recorded. It wasn't what I would call a hit, but its sound was more like what I thought to be really "me." Eddie Killroy, my new producer, had wanted to find and record the real Louise Mandrell. Previously, because I had felt that people might have been looking for Barbara's little sister, I hadn't felt quite comfortable with my sound. Now, I felt I was getting close to having my own style, and I think the fans and disc jockeys were feeling that, too.

Less than six months after the final taping of our television show, I was *ready* to record a hit song. I believed that my road show had progressed to the point where I could support one. I was very comfortable onstage and in handling interviews. In simple words, I was now a confident entertainer. It was time to round out my career with some success on the charts.

Eddie and RCA apparently agreed and spent countless hours searching for the right song for me to release next. When they found it, they allowed me to work as many hours in the studio as I needed to get it done *my way*. The song was entitled, "Some of My Best Friends Are Old Songs." It was a beautiful song, and the title was a statement with which I could really identify.

"Best Friends" did much better than anything else I had ever released. It was a Top Ten song in many local markets, and even hit number one in a few places. It wasn't a "monster" hit, but it did give me a taste of recording success and was another good step.

I enjoyed having fans request one of my songs that they loved. I was now more motivated than ever to become a success, and the press showed a new interest in my career also. It is amazing what one record can do!

TV's most beautiful drummer
(NBC photo)

The world's new interest in me, and my own new even deeper motivation, kept me working harder than ever. The success that I had tasted kept my spirits up during times when I was exhausted.

After all those times that I had worried about Barbara's not getting enough rest and working too hard, here I was working all the time and sleeping in short bursts. When I wasn't recording, I was doing shows; when I wasn't somewhere doing a show, I was doing a promotional tour. Every night I was in a different city. Though I had observed my sister at the same point in her career, it really hadn't prepared me for the pressures and demands. Still in this business, you have to make hay while the sun shines, and I just had to forget about being tired and forge ahead. After all, the audience had paid hard-earned money to see me at my best, and my *best* was exactly what I was going to give them.

The summer of '82 was spent on the road. The only way I could keep up with my family was by telephone, and even that almost always was a challenge. Irlene was touring fairs and amusement parks with the same Krofft Puppets we had used on our television show, and Barbara was working fairs, rodeos, and showrooms just like I was. Daddy was usually with Barbara, so the only person I knew I could find on a regular basis was Mom . . . she was holding down the office. To get in touch with any member of my family, I called Mom first and got the number. If I were lucky, the person I wanted was still at that number. Many times, though, we missed connections.

With our hectic road pacing, the only ways to keep harmony on the bus was to play games and have some fun. When you are traveling with nine or ten people confined within a limited area, even good friends who have worked together for years can get on one another's nerves. In order to give each of us breathing space, and to work off energy, at least once a day we would try to find a place to play softball. This had been a tradition for years with my band and is always a time we really enjoy—except the day when I blocked home plate to keep R.C. from scoring a winning run. He attempted to slide under my tag, and I caught an elbow to the jaw, which cost me fifteen stitches in my chin, but he was still out! Yes, softball is a great release for tension. But it's not our only release.

In July, in Nampa Valley, Idaho, we had our first real day off in weeks and decided to take full advantage of it. We had all heard about the fabulous white-water rafting on the Payette River in the Sawtooth Wilderness Area and wanted to give it a try.

Sawtooth Wilderness is one of the most beautiful and unspoiled tributes to nature I have ever seen. It is rugged and fierce, yet, at the same time, peaceful and serene. The river is a swirling mass of white water and rock. Its untamed, almost untouched state made me feel very close to heaven.

My nephew Matt had flown out to join us for a week. He may have been the real reason I signed up for this raft trip. I wanted to show him a good time and give him a new experience.

With the band along we had too many people to ride in just one raft, so we hired two guides and two rafts. R.C., Kelly (R.C.'s niece and my secretary), Matt, and I climbed in the first raft.

Floating down the river, being splashed by water, bobbing and weaving around rocks, and swirling in whirlpools was a thrill a second. This natural adventure brought forth the kinds of feelings man has often attempted in vain to duplicate with amusement park rides. It was an emotional rush and an emotional release—an opportunity to live life one second at a time, to feel and experience each breath of air and every heartbeat. The river ride took away all previous concerns and all future worries. It left my mind free to enjoy each moment.

I don't think that I have ever been as exhilarated in my entire life. My body was pushed up and down, back and forth, with each change of course taken by the river. Suddenly we hit a drop so severe that I actually left my seat and once again felt a cold burst of water coat my entire body. But the cold water didn't recede this time. I then realized I was out of the raft and underwater. I waited for my life jacket to float me to the top, but it didn't. I just swirled around and around, going no deeper, but rising no higher.

Probably only a second or two passed before I realized I was underwater, yet it seemed much longer. I flailed my arms, trying to swim to the surface, but I couldn't get from underneath whatever was holding me down. Frantically, I pushed and kicked, but I went nowhere. Panic seized me; I was trapped. Then I understood that the raft itself had me stuck. It either was caught in the same whirlpool I was, or the

R.C. and I joined RCA in 1981

guide was holding it in place in order to search for me. I was powerless to help myself. My heart sank. I knew I was doomed.

I was exhausted, but my fear had dissipated. If anything, I was truly at peace, I quit noticing my head hitting the bottom of the raft, and the water didn't feel cold any more. The river, which had been roaring in my ears, now seemed silent. I was alone; I knew that I was dying. My lungs quit struggling for air, and my eyes gave up the search for sunlight. I was drifting, my soul ready for quiet times and peace. It was almost as though I were welcoming what lay ahead. A few moments before everything had been loud and frantic, now all was quiet and still.

My mind didn't recognize the second I bobbed to the surface, but my lungs did—gasping for the life-giving air. My mind may have still been in its watery grave, but my body struggled to live again. I then felt R.C.'s strong arm sweep me out of the river and back into the raft, and I slowly

She is so beautiful

became aware that the people on the bank a few hundred feet away were cheering. I could only think: *It must have been quite a show! I just hope they don't want an encore!*

I later learned that I had been freed from the raft's hold because of our guide's maneuvering of our raft. My fighting had helped hold me in place, but when I had relaxed, the water actually carried me away from the raft and, like a giant hand, delivered me to the surface. The water that had exhilarated me then saved me, all in the same day. Thanks to that and our guide's intelligent navigation, I was alive.

The peace that I had felt while trapped under the raft was my last moment of real quiet for some time. With the success of "Some of My Best Friends Are Old Songs," and the even faster movement of my new single, "Romance," I was busier than ever. Every day, and almost every minute, I was working. Planes and buses were my home; I was on the move so much that I sometimes had to look at the telephone book in the motel room just to remember where I was. My public time was now all the time I had. If I did have a private moment, I was usually in a daze because everything was moving so quickly. My half-hour each day set aside just for me had been lost and was now just a memory.

When I did get to stop, I was overwhelmed with fatigue. Coupled with that feeling was the inability to drop right off to sleep, because I did not have a chance to stop and unwind. My mind was whirling. When the lights were off, I couldn't help getting frustrated over not being able to sleep, and this in itself kept me awake, too. Exhausted, eyes often wide open, I would almost invariably end up thinking about all that I had to do the next day. It was a never-ending circle. Still I wanted to press on. The drive that propelled Barbara was also pushing me.

I had to get up earlier in the morning now—I must look good before I went out . . . it was part of my career. Anything that would improve me, I wanted to do. I was determined to be a complete success, and I knew that sacrifice was the only way. Still I had moments during which I wondered if it was worth it. But down inside I knew I would not give up.

When your mind and body are exhausted, your perspective is not always perfect and can actually get slightly warped. During these times the most appealing answers are the short cuts, like pills and liquor. They offer a way to escape and rest, and as scared as I was of them, I could see that it would be easy to take that route and relax. Someone who is as tired as I was needs some other source of strength; you can't depend on just yourself.

My strength, though, comes from my family who is always there to give me love and security. R.C. became the force that kept understanding and communication open in our marriage. He gave up moments with me so that I could rest, and he pitched in and did many of my normal chores. When I needed it, he became my buffer to the outside world.

Barbara was great, too, calling me every day from wherever she was. She knew how I felt—she had felt that way for years. She helped me keep in touch with the real Louise Mandrell. When you're tired, you sometimes need to be reminded who you are.

Irlene would call and make me laugh. She has always been able to do that.

Finally my family and my friends didn't forget how to say no. I was surrounded by many people who thought everything that I did was great (or so they told me.) Therefore, I needed some people in my life who didn't tell me yes just to make me feel good—someone who would *not* laugh at my joke when it was not funny; someone to remind me that I was still human. They knew they couldn't slow me down, so they just kept my feet on the ground with their strength and honesty.

For years I had struggled to put together a stage show, sell records, and make a name for myself. Now it was falling together so quickly that it was overwhelming. Without my family's support I know that I would have been blown away and would have wasted the chance to see if there was room at the top for me. Their love and strength were giving me that chance.

Now I was answering many of the same questions Barbara had answered many times before. I was happy to realize that my answers were not the same, the media seemed to realize that we were different even though we were sisters with a close relationship. But there was no mistaking that our drive was the same.

As I read reviews and interviews I realized that *I* was now being called a sex symbol. It had taken me a while to get used to Barbara's being called that, but R.C. had been telling me for years that I was one, too. I adjusted quickly to this new view, but I also knew the label was just that—a label. Louise Mandrell stood for a lot of things, and if I could still present my true beliefs and feelings through my contacts with the public, I wasn't going to worry about a label.

In 1982 I learned that life and careers are to be taken very seriously. I had also grown to the point where I knew I had to continue to try to live up to what *I should be*, while continuing to read and hear all the things that writers, fans, and others said that I *was*. Thankfully, 1982 was the year in which I had become serious about my career, but had learned not to take myself too seriously.

And so it went one step at a time, and one day at a time—if I now have a philosophy of life, those two statements sum it up.

In 1982 the steps came faster and the days all began to run together. So many good things happened that I began to feel overly blessed. Despite all the hard work, and my fatigue, I had received great rewards—not only financially, but in growing confidence and acceptance and the knowledge that I was doing what I had been born to do. On a day-to-day basis, I felt satisfied with both myself and my career.

Bringing the show home with
gospel (NBC photo)

A new challenge was offered in 1983. Since we would not be recording together anymore, there was no strong reason for R.C. to be in my road show. Our last record had been a Christmas song he had written just for us—"Christmas Is Just a Song for Us This Year." It had sold more records than any of our previous recordings, but instead of a signal of future things, it served as a farewell to that facet of the business for R.C.

R.C. was now committing his life to doing what he wanted to . . . songwriting. He could not devote himself to this art while doing a full-time job somewhere else, so now that I had the confidence to stand on my own, he stepped back and pushed me forward—just as Barbara had done a few years before. The spotlight was all mine, and I would have to fill it on my own. My husband knew that I could do it.

I was happy that R.C. could now plunge back into the craft which I knew was his first love. While touring with me he had written some great hit songs. Now he could write more and better material and be recognized as what he truly wanted to be . . . a great writer.

R.C.'s leaving the show was anything but a surprise. We had discussed and planned this move for a long time. We had even spent hours with Joe Galante, RCA's top man in country music. Joe is very young, very bright, and a natural leader. He is also honest and loyal, and he had our complete trust. Because Joe thought too much of R.C. to keep him on the label just for the good of the label, he wanted R.C. to accept his life's calling. Not only that, but Joe assured R.C. that he too knew that I was now ready to be recognized by the label as a "great solo talent."

Joe's faith assured R.C. of RCA's confidence in me. We knew Joe believed that R.C. and I were both on the threshold of successful careers. Yet it would take me a little while to get used to Louise Mandrell's not having her R.C. onstage with her. I had learned much about showmanship from him. Writing's gain would be the stage's loss. I was both happy and sad.

Aunt Linda Mandrell (between R.C. and me), R.C.'s father and mother, Herman and Bea (behind Aunt Linda), and others in our "supporting cast"—R.C.'s family

The next step had been a long time coming . . . I was releasing a solo album. RCA now had the faith to give me a chance at the album market. They backed me with superior production, fantastic promotion, and sincere belief. They also marketed me as Louise Mandrell, recording artist and entertainer. I had never tried to escape Barbara's shadow and had waited to be recognized as a separate talent (who just happened to be Barbara Mandrell's sister and biggest fan). That time had now arrived.

When I started on my own, I played very small places and before very small crowds. I had loved that because the intimate contact had allowed me to get to know my audience and myself. Now I was playing large auditoriums and showrooms. I was working Atlantic City, Reno, and Las Vegas. I was working for audiences who were accustomed to the best and being seen by critics who had reviewed show business legends. I was hungry for this challenge, and I felt I was ready.

A few years before, all of these things had been dreams. Now they were real. More dreams were in front of me, waiting for me to grab and claim as my own. A new single, "Save Me," had become a big national hit; and I was to do my own TV special, and Barbara and Irlene were to be two of my guests. I had come too far and was too close to my goal to stop now. Every day I had to reach just a little bit higher. I wanted to go as far as I could. I needed to find my ultimate limits.

I guess that all of us girls are like that. Irlene is in Los Angeles with Daddy managing her career from Nashville. She is reading scripts for movies and is immersing herself in acting lessons. Music is strictly for fun now. She is pushing in a different direction and reaching for different goals from the rest of us.

Barbara has by now received almost every award and honor that can be bestowed on a country music entertainer, and many outside that category. She has played all the major cities and has performed for several presidents. She has become one of the world's best-known personalities. She released a gospel album that received rave reviews (not to mention a Grammy!)—not only for its production, but for its message. Still she reaches out to conquer new goals. Barbara's only limits are her principles.

We are all reaching, but in slightly different directions. And we still have our parents behind us. It must have been frustrating for them to watch me jump in and out of music, making mistakes, and stumbling. After all, Barbara had been so steady and sure. She had made very few missteps and mistakes. She had taken a very high road indeed. Yet never once did they ask me to be like my sister; they only wanted me to be me. Barbara and I are in the same field, but we each are different, and we got where we are in different ways. My parents are the reason for that.

In Irlene's case they had to deal with someone whose dreams were not of music, who almost always found the funny side of life when the rest of us were worried about business. So, Irlene was encouraged to develop the traits that made her different. Now she is using them in her acting.

The future is not promised to any of us, so I have no long-range goals or plans. I just want to continue to grow and expand my capacities to perform, to think, and to love to the fullest. I know that the best for all of us is yet to come. I can hardly wait to see what is on the next page of the Mandrell Family Album.

I want to thank the following for their
help and contributions.

Rheda Anderson Jones
Alice Wernigk
Billy R. Jones
Jeannie Ghent
Kathy Collins
CBS/Epic
RCA
MCA
NBC
Mandrell Management
Krofft Entertainment
Dick Blake International

—L.M.

DISCOLOGY

BARBARA MANDRELL SINGLES

Title	Label	Catalog #	Release Date
I've Been Lovin' You Too Long/ Baby, Come Home	Columbia	444955	7/22/69
Playing Around With Love/ I Almost Lost My Mind	Columbia	445143	4/14/70
Do-Right-Woman, Do-Right-Man/ The Letter	Columbia	445307	12/31/70
Treat Him Right/ Break My Mind	Columbia	445391	5/20/71
Tonight My Baby's Coming Home/ He'll Never Take the Place of You	Columbia	445505	11/4/71
Show Me/ Satisfied	Columbia	45580	3/17/72
Holdin' on (to the Love I Got)/ Smile, Somebody Loves You	Columbia	45702	9/22/72
Give a Little, Take a Little/ Ain't It Good	Columbia	45819	3/16/73

The Midnight Oil/			
In the Name of Love	Columbia 45904		7/13/73
This Time I Almost Made It/			
Son-of-a-Gun	Columbia 46054		5/17/74
Standing Room Only/			
Can't Help But Wonder	Dot/ABC 17601		11/75
That's What Friends Are for/			
The Beginning of the End	Dot/ABC 17623		3/76
Love Is Thin Ice/			
Will We Ever Make Love in			
Love Again?	Dot/ABC 17644		7/76
Midnight Angel/			
I Count You	Dot/ABC 17668		11/76
Married, But Not to Each Other/			
Fool's Gold	Dot/ABC 17688		3/8/77
Hold Me/			
This Is Not Another Cheatin'			
Song	Dot	17716	8/77
Woman to Woman/			
Let the Rain Out	Dot	17736	11/77
Tonight/			
If I Were a River	ABC	12362	4/6/78
Sleeping Single in a Double Bed/			
Just One More	ABC	12403	8/1/78
If Loving You Is Wrong,			
I Don't Want to Be Right/	ABC	12451	1/79
Fooled By a Feeling/			
Love Takes a Long Time			
to Die	MCA	41077	7/79
Years/			
Darlin'	MCA	41162	12/7/79
Crackers/			
Using Him to Get to You	MCA	41263	6/6/80
The Best of Strangers/			
Sometime, Somewhere,			
Somehow	MCA	51001	9/26/80
Love Is Fair/			
Sometime, Somewhere,			
Somehow	MCA	51062	1/23/81
I Was Country When Country			
Wasn't Cool/			

A Woman's Got a Right (to Change His Mind)	MCA	51107	4/16/81
Wish You Were Here/ She's out There Dancin' Along	MCA	51171	8/21/81
Till You're Gone/ You're Not Supposed to Be Here	MCA	52038	4/8/82
Operator/ Black and White	MCA	52111	8/12/82
In Times Like These/ Loveless	MCA	52206	3/28/83

BARBARA MANDRELL DUET SINGLES WITH DAVID HOUSTON

Title	Label	Catalog #	Release Date
After Closing Time/ My Song of Love	EPIC	5-10656	9/2/70
We've Got Everything But Love/ Try a Little Harder	EPIC	5-10779	8/23/71
A Perfect Match/ Almost Persuaded	EPIC	5-10908	8/16/72
I Love You, I Love You/ Let's Go Down Together	EPIC	5-11068	11/21/73
Lovin' You Is Worth It/ How Can It Be Wrong?	EPIC	5-11120	4/19/74
Ten Commandments of Love/ Try a Little Harder	EPIC	8-20005	7/12/74

BARBARA MANDRELL ALBUMS

Title	Label	Catalog #	Release Date
Treat Him Right	Columbia	C 30967	9/71
The Midnight Oil	Columbia	KC 32743	11/73

This Time I Almost Made It	Columbia	KC 32959	8/74
The Best of Barbara Mandrell	Columbia	PC 34876	8/77
Looking Back	Columbia	FC 37437	7/81
This Is Barbara Mandrell	Dot	DOSD-2045	1/76
Midnight Angel	Dot	DOSD-2067	9/76
Lovers, Friends, & Strangers	ABC/Dot	DO-2076	8/77
Love's Ups and Downs	ABC/Dot	DO-1098	3/78
Moods	ABC	AY-1088	9/78
The Best of Barbara Mandrell	ABC	AY-1119	3/79
Just for the Record	MCA	MCA-3165	7/79
Love Is Fair	MCA	MCA-5136	8/80
Barbara Mandrell Live	MCA	MCA-5243	8/81
In Black and White	MCA	MCA-5295	5/82
He Set My Life to Music	MCA/ Songbird	MCR-5023	9/82

BARBARA MANDRELL DUET ALBUMS WITH DAVID HOUSTON

Title	Label	Catalog #	Release Date
A Perfect Match	EPIC	KE 31705	8/72
The Best of Barbara Mandrell and David Houston	EPIC	KE 32915	4/74

LOUISE MANDRELL SINGLES

Title	Label	Catalog #	Release Date
Put It on Me/ Yes, I Do	EPIC		5/16/78
Everlasting Love/ You Never Cross My Mind	EPIC	8-50651	11/29/78
Everlasting Love/ Band of Gold	EPIC	28-50682	2/26/79
I Never Loved Anyone Like I Love You/ Surrender to My Heart	EPIC		7/11/79

Wake Me Up/			
That Song Called Forever	EPIC	9-50856	2/12/80
Beggin' for Mercy/			
Come Here	EPIC	9-50896	5/14/80
Love Insurance/			
When It Hurts You Most	EPIC	9-50935	8/18/80
(You Sure Know Your Way)			
Around My Heart/			
Dance Me Around, Cowboy	RCA	PB-13039	1/22/82
Some of My Best Friends Are			
Old Songs/			
689-Double-203	RCA	PB-13278	7/9/82
Romance/			
Better Things to Do	RCA	PB-13373	10/15/82
Save Me/			
Trust Me	RCA	PB-13450	2/11/82

LOUISE MANDRELL ALBUMS

Title	Label	Catalog #	Release Date
Louise Mandrell	EPIC	FE 37424	7/81
Close Up	RCA	MHL1-8601	1/83

LOUISE MANDRELL DUET SINGLES
WITH R.C. BANNON

Title	Label	Catalog #	Release Date
I Thought You'd Never Ask/			
Yes, I Do	EPIC	P-50668	1/23/79
Reunited/			
Hello There, Stranger	EPIC	50717	2/6/79
We Love Each Other/			
I Want to (Do Everything			
for You)	EPIC	50789	9/19/79

The Pleasure's All Mine/ One False Move (And I'm Yours)	EPIC	19-50951	10/14/81
Where There's Smoke, There's Fire/ Before You	RCA	PB-12359	12/23/81
Our Wedding Band/ Just Married	RCA	PB-13095	4/30/82
Christmas Is Just a Song For Us This Year	RCA	PB-13358	11/82

LOUISE MANDRELL DUET ALBUMS WITH R.C. BANNON

Title	Label	Catalog #	Release Date
Inseparable	EPIC	JE 36151	8/79
Love Won't Let Us Go	EPIC	JE 36759	10/80
Me and My R.C.	RCA	AHL1-4059	1/82
You're My Super Woman; You're My Incredible Man	RCA	AHL1-4377	9/82

R.C. BANNON SINGLES

Title	Label	Catalog #	Release Date
Southbound/ You Make All the Difference in the World	Columbia	3-10570	5/27/77
Rainbows and Horseshoes/ You Make All the Difference in the World	Columbia	10612	8/7/77
It Doesn't Matter Anymore/ All the Best	Columbia	10655	11/1/77
(The Truth Is) We're Living a Lie/ Love at First Sight	Columbia	10714	2/6/78

Loveless Motel/ Nightbird	Columbia	5/17/78

Somebody's Gonna Do It
  Tonight/
  Got That Lookin' Feelin'
	Columbia 10847	9/26/78

Winners and Losers/
  Cheatin' on Him, Lovin'
  on Me
	Columbia 11081	8/3/79

Lovely, Lonely Lady/ Ugly Woman	Columbia 1-11210	1/8/80
If You're Serious About Cheatin'/ What's a Nice Girl Like You	Columbia 1-11267	4/2/80
Never Be Anyone Else/ What's a Nice Girl Like You	Columbia 1-11346	7/28/80

Til Something Better Comes
  Along/
  You're Bringing out
  the Fool in Me
	RCA PB-13029	12/23/81

R.C. BANNON ALBUMS

Title	Label	Catalog #	Release Date
Have Some R.C.	Avra-Cee A-C 101		
R.C. Bannon Arrives	Columbia KC 35346		3/78

SPECIAL DATES
Birthdays

Irby	October 11
Mary	August 4
Barbara	December 25
Ken	July 23
Matthew	May 8
Jaime	February 23
Louise	July 13
R.C.	May 2
Irlene	January 29
Rick	May 15

Mary and Irby .... November 15
Barbara and Ken .... May 28
Louise and R.C... February 26
Irlene and Rick.. December 23

Louise Mandrell International Fan Club
P.O. Box 718
Antioch, TN 37013

Barbara Mandrell International Fan Club
P.O. Box 620
Hendersonville, TN 37075

BARBARA'S MAJOR AWARDS

1979

Female Vocalist of the Year, Country Music Association
Music City News, Best Female Vocalist
Female Entertainer of the Year, Cashbox Awards
Female Vocalist/Country Singles, Cashbox Awards
Female Vocalist of the Year, Radio & Records Awards
"Sleeping Single In A Double Bed," Single of the Year, *Billboard Magazine* and American Music Awards
Community Service Award, National Women Executives
Outstanding Artistic Achievement, Cashbox

1980

Entertainer of the Year, Country Music Association
Entertainer of the Year, Academy of Country Music
Billboard Magazine, Bill Williams Memorial Artist of the Year Award
Favorite Female Country Music Vocalist, American Music Awards
Country Style Magazine, Female Vocalist of Year

1981

Entertainer of the Year (second time), Country Music Association
Female Vocalist of the Year, Country Music Association

Top Female Vocalist of the Year, Academy of Country Music
Music City News, Female Vocalist of the Year
Music City News, Musician of the Year
Music City News, Best Comedy Act (Mandrell Sisters)
Music City News, Best TV Series (Barbara Mandrell & the Mandrell Sisters)
Billboard Magazine, Top Female Singles Artist
Record World Magazine, Top Female Vocalist
Entertainer of the Year, *Cashbox Magazine*
Favorite Female Country Music Vocalist, American Music Awards
Worst Dressed Woman, Mr. Blackwell

1982

Favorite All-Around Female Entertainer, People's Choice Awards
Favorite Female TV Personality, People's Choice Awards
Favorite Female Musical Performer, People's Choice Awards
Music City News, Female Vocalist of the Year
Music City News, Best TV Series (Barbara Mandrell & the Mandrell Sisters)
Music City News, Musician of the Year
Distinguished Tennessean of the Year, Tennessee Sports Hall of Fame
U.S. Magazine, Favorite Variety Star

1983

Elected to National Association for Sport and Physical Education Hall of Fame
Outstanding Mother of the Year, National Mother's Day Committee
Favorite All-Around Female Entertainer, People's Choice Awards
Favorite Female Country Vocalist, American Music Awards
Best Inspirational Performance, Grammy Award

LOUISE'S MAJOR AWARDS

1981

Music City News, Most Promising Female Vocalist
Music City News, TV Show of the Year
Music City News, Comedy Act of the Year
Texas Legislature enacted legislation naming her a "Yellow Rose of Texas"

1982

Music City News, TV Show of the Year
Tennessee City Managers' "Tennessee Sweetheart"

DANCE PARTNERS—"Barbara Mandrell and the Mandrell Sisters" TV SHOW

Vince Paterson
Ken Grant
Joey Sheck
Charles Ward

LOUISE MANDRELL'S "SPELLBOUND"

Rick King
Rusty Pence
Sam Grant
Steven Preston
Chris Peak
Keith McGregor
Jamie Walden
Pedro Tomas
Valerie McGregor
Janet Townson
Dan Waters
Han (Bubba) Henze
Kevin Heffelman

BARBARA MANDRELL'S "DO-RITES"

Lonnie Webb
Gary Smith
Gene Miller
Randy Wright
Lonny Hayes
Charles Bundy
Mike Jones

More Biography and Autobiography from SIGNET

(0451)

- [ ] **THE LOVE YOU MAKE: AN INSIDER'S STORY OF THE BEATLES** by Peter Brown and Steven Gaines. (127978—$4.50)*

- [ ] **THE UNOFFICIAL EDDIE MURPHY SCRAPBOOK** by Judith Davis. (128958—$2.50)*

- [ ] **BOB DYLAN** by Anthony Scaduto with an Introduction by Steven Gaines. (092899—$2.50)*

- [ ] **UP & DOWN WITH THE ROLLING STONES** by Tony Sanchez. (126637—$3.95)

- [ ] **FONDA: MY LIFE** as told to Howard Teichmann. (118588—$3.95)*

- [ ] **BOGIE** by Joe Hyams. (091892—$1.75)

- [ ] **KATE: THE LIFE OF KATHERINE HEPBURN** by Charles Higham. (112121—$2.95)*

- [ ] **FIRST, YOU CRY** by Betty Rollin. (112598—$2.50)

- [ ] **IF YOU COULD SEE WHAT I HEAR** by Tom Sullivan and Derek Gill. (118111—$2.75)*

- [ ] **W.C. FIELDS: HIS FOLLIES AND FORTUNES** by Robert Lewis Taylor. (506537—$1.25)

*Prices slightly higher in Canada

Buy them at your local

bookstore or use coupon

on next page for ordering.

More SIGNET Titles You'll Enjoy

(0451)

☐ **BERNARD MELTZER'S GUIDANCE FOR LIVING** by Bernard Meltzer.
(127730—$2.95)*

☐ **EVERY LOVING GIFT** by Judy Polikoff as told to Michele Sherman.
(127722—$3.50)*

☐ **SUPER NATURAL LIVING** by Betty Malz. (125177—$2.50)*

☐ **PRAYERS THAT ARE ANSWERED** by Betty Malz. (119916—$2.50)

☐ **LADY ON THE RUN** by Lucille Schirman. (118316—$2.75)*

☐ **CELEBRATE JOY!** by Velma Seawell Daniels. (119452—$2.50)*

☐ **MY SHADOW RAN FAST** by Bill Sands. (098714—$2.25)

☐ **OPEN HEART, OPEN HOME** by Karen Burton Mains. (095308—$1.95)*

☐ **THE NIGHT THEY BURNED THE MOUNTAIN** by Dr. Tom Dooley.
(086813—$1.50)

☐ **GOD'S SMUGGLER** by Brother Andrew with J. and E. Sherrill
(098684—$2.25)

☐ **LETTER TO A YOUNGER SON** by Christopher Leach. (119207—$2.25)*
*Prices slightly higher in Canada.

SIGNET Books of Related Interest

**Buy them at your local
bookstore or use coupon
on next page for ordering.**

Quintessential Quiz Books from SIGNET

More Bestsellers from SIGNET

*Prices slightly higher in Canada

**Buy them at your local
bookstore or use coupon
on next page for ordering.**

More Bestsellers From SIGNET